THE BARBECUE BOOK

THE BARBECUE BOOK

CLASSIC RECIPES FOR THE BARBECUE AND OUTDOOR GRILL

CHRISTINE FRANCE

Sebastian Kelly

Paperback edition published by
Sebastian Kelly
2 Rectory Road, Oxford OX4 1BW

Produced by Anness Publishing Limited
Hermes House, 88–89 Blackfriars Road, London SE1 8HA

ISBN 1-84081-207-9

Publisher: Joanna Lorenz
Editor: Sarah Ainley
Copy Editor: Beverley Jollands
Designer: Nigel Partridge
Cover Design: Clare Baggaley
Illustrations: Madeleine David and Lucinda Ganderton
Photographers: William Adams-Lingwood, Steve Baxter, John Freeman, Michelle Garrett, Amanda Heywood, Michael Michaels and Patrick McLeavey
Recipes: Carla Capalbo, Jacqueline Clark, Carole Clements, Nicola Diggins, Tessa Evelegh, Joanna Farrow, Christine France, Ruby Le Bois and Katherine Richmond

Previously published as part of a larger compendium, *The Ultimate Barbecue Cookbook*

Printed and bound in Singapore

1 3 5 7 9 10 8 6 4 2

Contents

Introduction 6

Appetizers and Snacks 14

Meat Dishes 30

Poultry and Game 58

Fish and Seafood 80

Vegetarian Dishes and Vegetables 104

Salads and Accompaniments 122

Salsas, Dips and Marinades 132

Desserts 146

Index 159

Introduction

However simple, there's something about the charbroiled flavor of barbecued food that makes it taste extra special. Maybe it owes part of its appeal to the fresh air that sharpens the appetite and makes that tantalizing aroma so totally irresistible.

There's nothing new about cooking over charcoal; in fact, it's a method of cooking that has been used in most civilizations throughout history. The basic method has changed little over the centuries, but many modern grills are very sophisticated, making the job easier, cleaner and more controllable. Whether you're cooking over a simple pile of sticks or on a state-of-the art gas grill, outdoor cooking is fun, easy and inexpensive.

There are disputes over the origin of the word "barbecue," but one explanation is that it comes from *barbacoa*, a Spanish-American word used by the Arawak tribe of the Caribbean as the name for the wooden frame that held their food over an open fire as it cooked. The Arawaks were cannibals, so the food we cook today is rather different from their offerings!

Whatever your tastes, this collection of recipes offers new, unusual ideas for your barbecue as well as some traditional favorites. There's something for every occasion, from family meals to entertaining: spicy, fruity and exotic grills using fish, meat and poultry; easy sauces and marinades to turn basic ingredients into something new and special; and luscious, indulgent desserts. For vegetarians, there's a whole chapter of innovative ideas that everyone will enjoy.

Best of all, not only does a barbecue set the cook free from the kitchen but, for once, everyone else will actually want to help with the cooking.

Choosing a Grill

There is a huge choice of ready-made grills on the market, and it's important to choose one that suits your particular needs. First decide how many people you want to cook for and where you are likely to use the grill. For instance, do you usually have barbecues just for the family, or are you likely to have barbecue parties for lots of friends? Once you've decided on your basic requirements, you will be able to choose between the different types more easily.

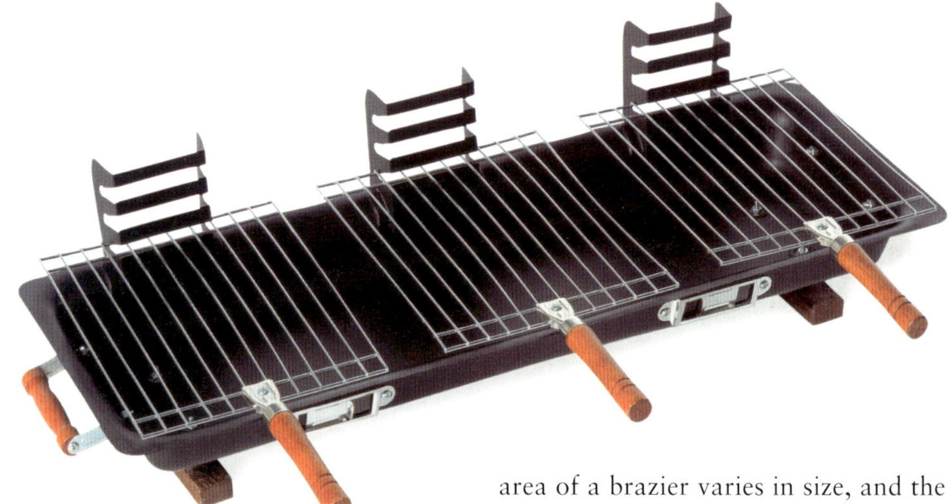

ABOVE: *Hibachis*

Hibachis

These small cast-iron grills originated in Japan—the word *hibachi* translates literally as "firebox." They are inexpensive, easy to use and easily transportable. Lightweight versions are now made in steel or aluminum.

Disposable Grills

These will last for about an hour and are a convenient idea for picnic-style barbecues or for cooking just a few small pieces of food.

Portable Grills

These are usually quite light and fold away to fit into a car trunk so you can take them on picnics. Some are even small enough to fit into a backpack.

Brazier Grills

These open grills are suitable for use on a patio or in the garden. Most have legs or wheels, and it's a good idea to check that the height suits you. The grill area of a brazier varies in size, and the brazier may be round or rectangular. It's useful to choose one that has a shelf attached to the side. Other extras may include an electric, battery-powered or clockwork spit: Choose one on which you can adjust the height of the spit. Many brazier grills have a hood, which is useful as a windbreak and gives a place to mount the spit.

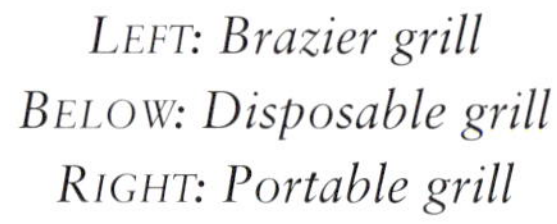

LEFT: *Brazier grill*
BELOW: *Disposable grill*
RIGHT: *Portable grill*

Above: Gas grill

Kettle Grills

These have a large, hinged lid, which can be used as a windbreak; when closed, the lid allows you to use the grill rather like an oven. Even large cuts of meat or whole turkeys cook successfully, as the heat reflected within the dome helps to brown the meat evenly. The heat is easily controlled by the use of efficient air vents. This type of grill can also be used for home-smoking foods.

Gas Grills

The main advantage of these is their convenience—the heat is instant and easily controllable. The disadvantage is that they tend to be quite expensive.

Permanent Grills

These are a good idea if you often have barbecues at home. They can be built simply and cheaply. Choose a sheltered site that is a little way from the house, but with easy access to the kitchen. Permanent grills can be built with ordinary house bricks, but it's best to line the inside with firebricks, which will withstand the heat better. Use a metal shelf for the fuel and a grid at whatever height you choose. Kits are available containing all you need to build a grill.

Improvised Grills

Barbecue cooking adds to the fun of eating outdoors on picnics and camping trips but transporting the grill for the rest of the day can make the idea more of a chore than a treat. Basic grills can be built at almost no cost and can be dismantled after use as quickly as they were put together. A pile of stones topped with chicken wire and fueled with driftwood or kindling makes a very efficient grill. Or take a large cookie tin with you and punch a few holes in it; fill it with charcoal and place a grid on top. With just a little planning, you can turn your trip into a truly memorable event.

Above: Improvised grill

Above: Permanent grill

Types of Fuel

If you have a gas or electric grill, you will not need to buy extra fuel, but other grills require either charcoal or wood. Be sure to choose good quality fuel and always remember to store it in a dry place.

Lump Charcoal

Lump charcoal is usually made from softwood and comes in lumps of varying size. It is easier to ignite than briquettes, but tends to burn up faster.

Charcoal Briquettes

Briquettes are a cost-effective choice of fuel, as they burn for a long time with a minimum of smell and smoke. They can take a long time to ignite, however.

LIGHTING THE FIRE

Follow these basic instructions for lighting the fire unless you are using self-igniting charcoal, in which case you should follow the manufacturer's instructions.

1 Spread a layer of foil over the base of the grill, to reflect the heat and make cleaning easier.

2 Spread a layer of wood, charcoal or briquettes on the fire grate about two inches deep. Pile the fuel in a small pyramid in the center.

3 Push one or two lighters into the fuel or pour about three tablespoons of lighting fluid over it and let sit for 1 minute. Light with a long match or taper and allow to burn for 15 minutes. Spread the coals evenly and leave them to heat for 30–45 minutes, until they are covered with a film of gray ash, before cooking.

ABOVE: Charcoal briquettes

Self-igniting Charcoal

This is simply lump charcoal or briquettes treated with a flammable substance that catches fire very easily. It's important to wait until the ignition agent has burned off before cooking food, or the smell may taint the food.

Coconut-shell Charcoal

This makes a good fuel for small grills. It's best used on a fire grate with small holes, as the small pieces tend to fall through the gaps.

Wood

Hardwoods such as oak and olive are best for grilling, as they burn slowly, with a pleasant aroma. Softwoods tend to burn too fast and give off sparks and smoke, making them unsuitable for most grills. Wood fires need constant attention to achieve an even, steady heat.

BELOW: Lump charcoal

CONTROLLING THE HEAT

There are three basic ways to control the heat of the grill during cooking.

1 Adjust the height of the grill rack. Raise it for slow cooking, or use the bottom level for searing foods. For medium heat, the rack should be about four inches from the fire.

2 Push the burning coals apart for lower heat; pile them closer together to increase the heat of the fire.

3 Most grills have air vents to allow air into the fire. Open them to make the fire hotter, or close them to lower the temperature.

Wood Chips and Herbs

These are designed to be added to the fire to impart a pleasant aroma to the food. They can be soaked to make them last longer. Scatter wood chips and herbs straight onto the coals during cooking, or place them on a metal tray under the grill rack. Packs of hickory or oak chips are easily available, or you can simply scatter twigs of juniper, rosemary, thyme, sage or fennel over the fire.

BELOW: Coconut-shell charcoal

SAFETY TIPS

Barbecuing is a perfectly safe method of cooking if it's done sensibly—use these simple guidelines as a basic checklist to safeguard against accidents. If you have never organized a barbecue before, keep your first few attempts as simple as possible, with just one or two types of food. When you have mastered the technique of cooking on a grill you can start to become more ambitious. Soon you will progress from burgers for two to meals for large parties of family and friends.

☆ Make sure the grill is sited on a firm surface and is stable and level before lighting the fire. Once the grill is lit, do not move it.

☆ Keep the grill sheltered from the wind, and keep it well away from trees and shrubs.

☆ Always follow the manufacturer's instructions for your grill, as there are some grills that can use only one type of fuel.

☆ Don't try to speed up the fire—some fuels may take a long time to build up heat. Never pour flammable liquid onto the grill.

☆ Keep children and pets away from the fire and make sure the cooking is always supervised by adults.

☆ Keep perishable foods cold until you're ready to cook—especially in hot weather. If you take them outdoors, place them in a cool bag until needed.

☆ Make sure meats such as burgers, sausages and poultry are thoroughly cooked—there should be no trace of pink in the juices. Pierce a thick part of flesh as a test: the juices should run clear.

RIGHT: Poultry can be precooked in the oven or microwave before being finished off on the grill

ABOVE: Light the fire with a long match or taper, and leave it to burn for about 15 minutes

☆ Wash your hands after handling raw meat and before touching other foods. Don't use the same utensils for raw ingredients and cooked food.

☆ You may prefer to precook poultry in the microwave or oven and then transfer it to the grill to finish cooking and to attain the flavor of barbecued food. Don't allow meat to cool down before transferring it to the grill; poultry should never be reheated once it has already cooled.

☆ In case the fire should get out of control, have a bucket of sand and a water spray on hand to douse the flames.

☆ Keep a first-aid kit handy. If someone gets burned, hold the burn under cold running water.

☆ Trim excess fat from meat and don't use too much oil in marinades. Fat can cause dangerous flare-ups if too much is allowed to drip onto the fuel.

☆ Use long-handled grilling tools, such as forks, tongs and brushes, for turning and basting food; keep some oven gloves nearby, preferably the extra-long type, to protect your hands.

☆ Always keep the raw foods to be cooked away from foods that are ready to eat, to prevent cross-contamination.

BASIC TIMING GUIDE

It is almost impossible to give precise timing guides for barbecuing, as there are so many factors to consider. The heat will depend on the type and size of the grill, the type of fuel used, the height of the rack above the fire and, of course, the weather. Cooking times will also be affected by the thickness and type of food, the quality of the meat, and where on the grill it is placed.

Bearing this in mind, the chart below provides only a rough guide to timing. Food should always be tested to make sure it is thoroughly cooked. The times given here are total cooking times, allowing for the food to be turned. Most foods need turning only once, but smaller items, such as kebabs and sausages, need to be turned more frequently to ensure even cooking. Foods wrapped in foil cook more slowly and will need longer on the grill.

Type of Food	Weight/ Thickness	Heat	Total Cooking Time
Beef			
steaks	1 inch	hot	rare: 5 minutes medium: 8 minutes well done: 12 minutes
burgers	¾ inch	hot	6–8 minutes
kebabs	1 inch	hot	5–8 minutes
roasts	3½ pounds	spit	2–3 hours
Lamb			
leg steaks	¾ inch	medium	10–15 minutes
chops	1 inch	medium	10–15 minutes
kebabs	1 inch	medium	6–15 minutes
butterfly leg	3 inches	low	rare: 40–45 minutes well done: 1 hour
rolled shoulder	3½ pounds	spit	1¼–1½ hours
Pork			
chops	1 inch	medium	15–18 minutes
kebabs	1 inch	medium	12–15 minutes
spareribs		medium	30–40 minutes
sausages	thick	medium	8–10 minutes
roasts	3½ pounds	spit	2–3 hours

Type of Food	Weight/ Thickness	Heat	Total Cooking Time
Chicken			
whole	3½ pounds	spit	1–1¼ hours
quarters		medium	30–35 minutes
boneless breasts		medium	10–15 minutes
drumsticks		medium	25–30 minutes
kebabs		medium	6–10 minutes
poussin, whole	1 pound	spit	25–30 minutes
poussin, split	1 pound	medium	25–30 minutes
Duckling			
whole	5 pounds	spit	1–1½ hours
half		medium	35–45 minutes
breasts, boneless		medium	15–20 minutes
Fish			
large, whole	5–10 pounds	low/ medium	allow 10 minutes per 1 inch thickness
small, whole	1¼–2 pounds	hot/ medium	12–20 minutes
sardines		hot/ medium	4–6 minutes
steaks or fillets	1 inch	medium	6–10 minutes
kebabs	1 inch	medium	5–8 minutes
large shrimp in shell		medium	6–8 minutes
large shrimp, shelled		medium	4–6 minutes
scallops/mussels in shell		medium	until open
scallops/mussels, shelled, skewered		medium	5–8 minutes
half lobster		low/ medium	15–20 minutes

MARINATING

Marinades are used to add flavor and to moisten or tenderize foods, particularly meat. Marinades can be either savory or sweet and are as varied as you want to make them: spicy, fruity, fragrant or exotic. Certain classic combinations always work well with certain foods. Usually, it is best to choose oily marinades for dry foods, such as lean meat or white fish, and wine- or vinegar-based marinades for rich foods with a higher fat content. Most marinades don't contain salt, which can draw out the juices from meat. It's better to add salt just before, or after, cooking.

1 Place the food for marinating in a wide, nonmetallic dish or bowl, preferably a dish that is large enough to allow the food to lie in a single layer.

2 Mix together the ingredients for the marinade according to the recipe. The marinade can usually be prepared in advance and stored in a jar with a screw-top lid until needed.

Cook's Tip

The amount of marinade you will need depends on the amount of food. As a rough guide, about ⅔ cup is enough for about 1¼ pounds of food.

3 Pour the marinade over the food and turn the food to coat it evenly.

4 Cover the dish or bowl with plastic wrap and chill in the refrigerator for anywhere from 30 minutes up to several hours or overnight, depending on the recipe. Turn the food over occasionally, and spoon the marinade over it to make sure it is well coated.

5 Remove the food with a slotted spoon, or lift it out with tongs, and drain off and reserve the marinade. If necessary, allow the food to come to room temperature before cooking.

6 Use the marinade for basting or brushing the food during cooking.

BASIC BARBECUE MARINADE

This can be used for meat or fish.

1 garlic clove, crushed
3 tablespoons sunflower or olive oil
3 tablespoons dry sherry
1 tablespoon Worcestershire sauce
1 tablespoon dark soy sauce
freshly ground black pepper

RED WINE MARINADE

This is good with red meats and game.

⅔ cup dry red wine
1 tablespoon olive oil
1 tablespoon red wine vinegar
2 garlic cloves, crushed
2 dried bay leaves, crumbled
freshly ground black pepper

BELOW: *Marinating foods before cooking adds to the flavor and ensures the food is kept tender and moist*

Appetizers and Snacks

As everyone knows, there is nothing like the aroma of charbroiling food to whet the appetite. To keep your guests happy while they are waiting for the main event, begin your barbecue feast with exciting appetizers that are quick to cook and fun to eat. Here is a collection of flavorsome and colorful dishes that are guaranteed to disappear from the grill rack as soon as they're cool enough to snatch away. There are lots of creative recipes for finger foods to be nibbled with drinks – from crisp garlic toasts to spicy spare ribs – with plenty of interesting dips and sauces to dunk them in, as well as delicious suggestions for elegant appetizers for more formal meals.

ROASTED GARLIC TOASTS

Roasting garlic in its skin on a grill produces a soft, aromatic purée with a sweet, nutty flavor. Spread on crisp toast to make a delicious appetizer or accompaniment to meat or vegetable dishes.

INGREDIENTS

2 whole garlic heads
extra virgin olive oil
fresh rosemary sprigs
loaf of ciabatta or thick baguette
chopped fresh rosemary
salt and freshly ground black pepper

SERVES 4

1 Slice the tops from the heads of garlic using a sharp kitchen knife.

2 Brush the garlic heads with extra virgin olive oil and add a few sprigs of fresh rosemary before wrapping in foil. Cook the foil parcels on a medium-hot grill for 25–30 minutes, turning occasionally, until the garlic is soft.

3 Slice the bread and brush each slice generously with olive oil. Toast the slices on the grill until crisp and golden, turning once.

4 Squeeze the garlic cloves from their skins onto the toasts. Sprinkle with the chopped fresh rosemary and olive oil, and add salt and black pepper to taste.

ROASTED PEPPER ANTIPASTO

Jars of Italian mixed peppers in olive oil are a common sight in supermarkets, yet none can compete with this freshly made version, perfect as an appetizer or served with cold cuts.

INGREDIENTS

3 red bell peppers
2 yellow or orange bell peppers
2 green bell peppers
½ cup sun-dried tomatoes in oil, drained
1 garlic clove
2 tablespoons balsamic vinegar
5 tablespoons olive oil
few drops of chili sauce
4 canned artichoke hearts, drained and sliced
salt and freshly ground black pepper
fresh basil leaves, to garnish

SERVES 6

1 Cook the whole peppers on a medium-hot grill, turning frequently, for 10–15 minutes, until they begin to char. Cover the grilled peppers with a clean dish towel and allow them to cool for 5 minutes.

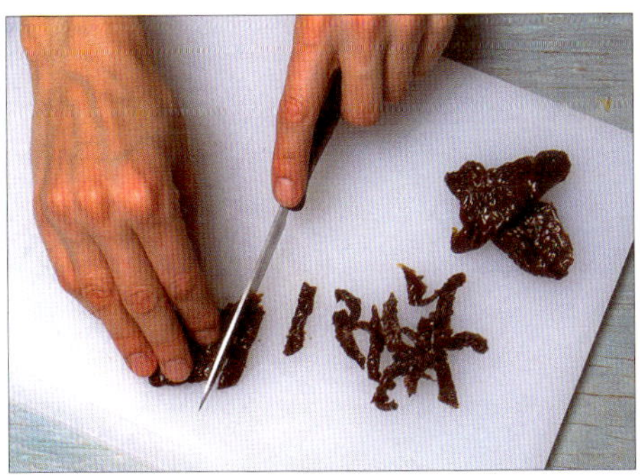

2 Use a sharp kitchen knife to slice the sun-dried tomatoes into thin strips. Thinly slice the garlic clove.

3 Whisk together the balsamic vinegar, olive oil and chili sauce in a small bowl, then season with a little salt and freshly ground black pepper.

4 Cut off the stalks and slice the peppers. Mix with the artichokes, sun-dried tomatoes and garlic. Add the dressing and sprinkle with basil leaves.

SPICY MEATBALLS

These meatballs are delicious served piping hot with chili sauce. Keep the sauce on the side so that everyone can add as much heat as they like.

2 Add the ground beef, shallots, garlic, bread crumbs, beaten egg and parsley, with plenty of salt and pepper. Mix well, then use your hands to shape the mixture into 18 small balls.

3 Brush the meatballs with olive oil and cook on a medium grill, or fry them in a large pan, for about 10–15 minutes, turning regularly until evenly browned and cooked through.

INGREDIENTS

4 ounces fresh spicy sausages
4 ounces ground beef
2 shallots, finely chopped
2 garlic cloves, finely chopped
1½ cups fresh white bread crumbs
1 egg, beaten
2 tablespoons chopped fresh parsley, plus extra to garnish
1 tablespoon olive oil
salt and freshly ground black pepper
Tabasco or other hot chili sauce, to serve

SERVES 6

1 Use your hands to remove the skins from the sausages, placing the sausage meat in a mixing bowl and breaking it up with a fork.

4 Transfer the meatballs to a warm dish and sprinkle with chopped fresh parsley. Serve with chili sauce.

CHORIZO IN OLIVE OIL

Spanish chorizo sausage has a deliciously pungent taste. Frying chorizo with onions and olive oil is one of the best ways of using it; you can also cook it on the grill, brushed with olive oil.

INGREDIENTS

5 tablespoons extra virgin olive oil
12 ounces chorizo sausage, sliced
1 large onion, thinly sliced
flat leaf parsley, roughly chopped, to garnish

SERVES 4

1 Heat the olive oil in a frying pan and fry the chorizo over high heat until beginning to color. Remove from the pan with a slotted spoon.

2 Add the onion slices to the pan and fry until golden. Return the sausage slices to the pan for about 1 minute to heat through.

3 Pour the mixture into a shallow serving dish and sprinkle with the chopped flat leaf parsley. Serve the chorizo on its own or as a side dish, with warm crusty bread.

Variation

Chorizo is usually available in large supermarkets and delicatessens, but any other similar spicy sausage can be used as a substitute.

Herb Polenta

Golden polenta made with fresh summer herbs and served with grilled tomatoes makes a tasty appetizer or light snack.

INGREDIENTS

3 cups stock or water
1 teaspoon salt
1 cup polenta
2 tablespoons butter
5 tablespoons mixed chopped fresh parsley, chives and basil, plus extra to garnish
olive oil for brushing
4 large plum or beef tomatoes, halved
salt and freshly ground black pepper

SERVES 4

1 Prepare the polenta in advance: Place the stock or water in a saucepan, with the salt, and bring to a boil. Reduce the heat and stir in the polenta.

2 Stir constantly over moderate heat for 5 minutes, until the polenta begins to thicken and come away from the sides of the saucepan.

3 Remove from the heat and stir in the butter, chopped herbs and pepper.

4 Lightly grease a wide pan or dish and pour the polenta into it, spreading it evenly. Set aside until cool and set.

5 Turn out the polenta and cut into squares or stamp out rounds with a large cookie cutter. Brush with olive oil. Lightly brush the tomatoes with oil and sprinkle with salt and pepper. Cook the tomatoes and polenta on a medium-hot grill for about 5 minutes, turning once. Serve garnished with fresh herbs.

Cook's Tip

Try using fresh basil or fresh chives alone, for a distinctive flavor.

BRIE PARCELS WITH ALMONDS

Creamy French Brie makes a sophisticated appetizer or light meal, wrapped in grape leaves and served hot with chunks of crusty bread.

INGREDIENTS

4 large grape leaves, in brine
7-ounce piece Brie cheese
2 tablespoons chopped fresh chives
2 tablespoons ground almonds
1 teaspoon crushed black peppercorns
1 tablespoon olive oil, plus extra for brushing
sliced almonds

SERVES 4

1 Rinse the grape leaves thoroughly under cold running water and dry them well. Spread the leaves out on a clean work surface or chopping board.

2 Cut the Brie into four chunks and place each chunk on a grape leaf.

3 Mix together the chives, ground almonds, peppercorns and olive oil, and place a spoonful on top of each piece of cheese. Sprinkle with sliced almonds.

4 Fold the grape leaves over tightly to enclose the cheese completely. Brush the parcels with olive oil and cook on a hot grill for 3–4 minutes, until the cheese is hot and melting. Serve immediately.

FIVE-SPICE RIB-STICKERS

To make these a real success, choose the meatiest spareribs you can find; remember to keep a supply of paper napkins within easy reach.

INGREDIENTS

2¼ pounds Chinese-style pork spareribs
2 teaspoons Chinese five-spice powder
2 garlic cloves, crushed
1 tablespoon grated fresh ginger
½ teaspoon chili sauce
4 tablespoons dark soy sauce
3 tablespoons dark brown sugar
1 tablespoon sunflower oil
4 scallions

SERVES 4

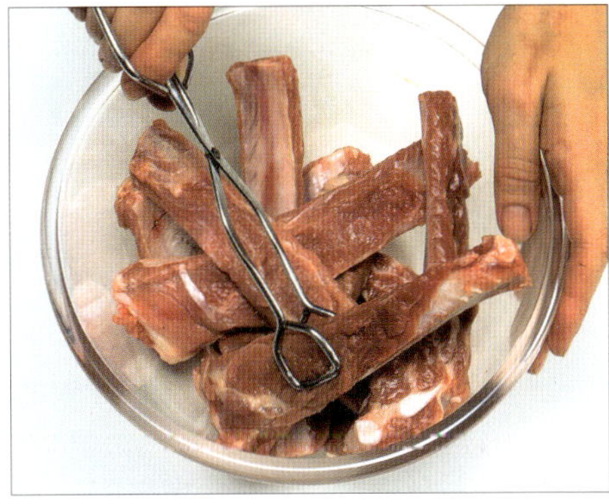

1 If the spareribs are still attached to each other, cut between them to separate them (or you could ask your butcher to do this when you buy them). Place the spareribs in a large bowl.

2 Mix together all the remaining ingredients except the scallions; pour this mixture over the ribs. Toss well to coat evenly. Cover the bowl and let marinate in the refrigerator overnight.

3 Cook the ribs on a medium-hot grill, turning frequently, for 30–40 minutes. Brush occasionally with the remaining marinade.

4 While the ribs are cooking, finely slice the scallions. Sprinkle them over the ribs and serve immediately.

CHICKEN WINGS TERIYAKI STYLE

This Japanese-style glaze is very simple to prepare and adds a unique flavor to the meat. The glaze can be used with any cut of chicken or with fish.

INGREDIENTS

1 garlic clove, crushed
3 tablespoons soy sauce
2 tablespoons dry sherry
2 teaspoons honey
2 teaspoons grated fresh ginger
1 teaspoon sesame oil
12 chicken wings
1 tablespoon sesame seeds, toasted

SERVES 4

1 Place the garlic, soy sauce, sherry, honey, grated ginger and sesame oil in a large bowl and beat with a fork, to mix the ingredients together evenly.

2 Add the chicken wings and toss thoroughly, to coat in the marinade. Cover the bowl with plastic wrap and chill for 30 minutes or longer.

3 Cook the chicken wings on a fairly hot grill for 20–25 minutes, turning occasionally and basting with the remaining marinade.

4 Sprinkle the chicken wings with sesame seeds. Serve the wings on their own as an appetizer or side dish, or as a light meal with a crisp green salad.

TOFU STEAKS

Vegetarians and meat-eaters alike will enjoy these barbecued tofu steaks. The combination of ingredients in the marinade gives the steaks a distinctly Japanese flavor.

INGREDIENTS

1 container fresh tofu (4 × 3¼ × 1¼ inches), 11 ounces drained weight
2 scallions, thinly sliced, to garnish
mixed salad leaves, to garnish

FOR THE MARINADE

3 tablespoons sake
2 tablespoons soy sauce
1 teaspoon sesame oil
1 garlic clove, crushed
1 tablespoon grated fresh ginger
1 scallion, finely chopped

SERVES 4

1 Wrap the tofu in a clean dish towel and place it on a chopping board. Put a large plate on top and let stand for 30 minutes to remove any excess water.

2 Slice the tofu horizontally into three pieces, then cut the slices into quarters. Set aside. Mix the ingredients for the marinade in a large bowl. Add the tofu to the bowl in a single layer and allow to marinate for 30 minutes. Drain the tofu steaks and reserve the marinade to use for basting.

3 Cook the steaks on the grill for 3 minutes on each side, basting regularly with the marinade, or fry them for 3 minutes in a large pan.

4 Arrange 3 tofu steaks on each plate. Any remaining marinade can be heated in a pan and then poured over the steaks. Sprinkle with the scallions and garnish with mixed salad leaves. Serve immediately.

Cook's Tip

Tofu is easily obtainable from supermarkets and health food stores, and is an ideal alternative to meat.

POLPETTE WITH MOZZARELLA AND TOMATO

These Italian-style meatballs are made with beef and topped with creamy melted mozzarella and savory anchovies.

INGREDIENTS

1/2 slice white bread, crusts removed
3 tablespoons milk
1 1/2 pounds ground beef
1 egg, beaten
2/3 cup dry bread crumbs
olive oil for brushing
2 beefsteak or other large tomatoes, sliced
1 tablespoon chopped fresh oregano
6 slices mozzarella cheese
6 canned anchovy fillets, drained and cut in half lengthwise
salt and freshly ground black pepper

SERVES 6

1 Put the bread and milk into a small saucepan and heat very gently, until the bread absorbs all the milk. Mash it to a pulp and set aside to cool.

2 Put the ground beef into a bowl with the bread mixture and the egg and season with plenty of salt and freshly ground black pepper. Mix well, then shape the mixture into 6 patties, using your hands. Sprinkle the bread crumbs onto a plate and dredge the patties, coating them thoroughly.

3 Brush the polpette with olive oil and cook them on a hot grill for 2–3 minutes on one side, until brown. Turn them over.

4 Without removing the polpette from the grill, lay a slice of tomato on top of each one, sprinkle with chopped oregano and season with salt and pepper. Place a mozzarella slice on top and arrange 2 strips of anchovy in a cross over the cheese.

5 Cook for another 4–5 minutes, until the polpette are cooked through and the mozzarella has melted.

SKEWERED LAMB WITH RED ONION SALSA

A simple salsa makes a refreshing accompaniment to this summery dish—make sure you use a mild-flavored red onion that is fresh and crisp, and a tomato that is ripe and full of flavor.

INGREDIENTS

8 ounces lean lamb, cubed
½ teaspoon ground cumin
1 teaspoon ground paprika
1 tablespoon olive oil
salt and freshly ground black pepper

FOR THE SALSA

1 red onion, very thinly sliced
1 large tomato, seeded and chopped
1 tablespoon red wine vinegar
3 or 4 fresh basil or mint leaves, roughly torn
small mint leaves, to garnish

SERVES 4

1 Place the lamb in a large bowl with the cumin, paprika and olive oil and season with plenty of salt and freshly ground black pepper. Toss well. Cover the bowl with plastic wrap and let sit in a cool place for several hours or in the refrigerator overnight, so that the lamb fully absorbs the spicy flavors.

2 Spear the lamb cubes on four small skewers. If using wooden skewers, soak them first in cold water for at least 30 minutes to prevent them from burning when placed on the grill.

3 To make the salsa, put the sliced onion, tomato, red wine vinegar and torn fresh basil or mint leaves in a small bowl and stir together until thoroughly blended. Season to taste with salt and garnish with mint.

4 Cook the skewered lamb on a hot grill or under a hot broiler for 5–10 minutes, turning the skewers frequently, until the lamb is well browned but still slightly pink in the center. Serve hot, with the salsa.

CIABATTA WITH MOZZARELLA AND ONIONS

Ciabatta, a crusty, flavorful Italian bread, is even more delicious when made with spinach, sun-dried tomatoes or olives: You can find these variations in many supermarkets.

INGREDIENTS

1 loaf of ciabatta
4 tablespoons red pesto
2 small onions
olive oil, for brushing
8 ounces mozzarella cheese, sliced
8 black olives, halved and pitted

MAKES 4

1 Cut the bread in half horizontally and toast the cut sides lightly on the grill. Spread with the pesto.

2 Peel the onions and cut them horizontally into slices. Brush with oil and cook on a hot grill for 4–5 minutes, until caramelized.

3 Arrange the cheese slices on the bread. Add the onion slices and scatter some olives on top. Cut in half. Return to the grill or broiler to melt the cheese.

CROSTINI WITH TOMATO AND ANCHOVY

Crostini are little rounds of bread cut from a baguette and crisply toasted, then covered with a topping, such as this savory mixture of tomato and anchovy.

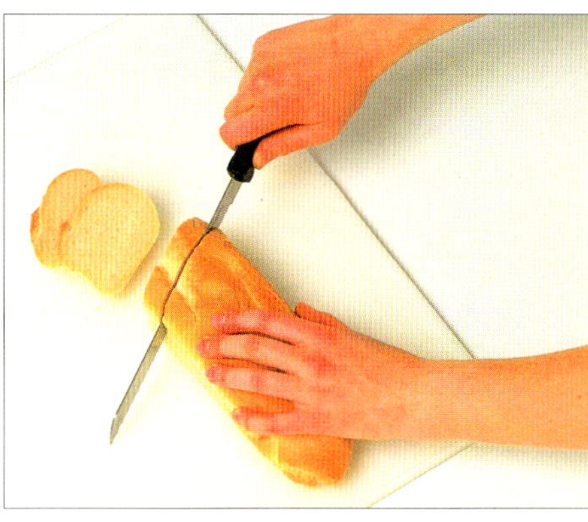

2 Cut the bread diagonally into 8 slices about ½-inch thick and brush with the remaining oil. Toast on the grill until golden, turning once.

3 Spoon a little of the tomato mixture onto each slice of bread. Place an anchovy fillet on each one and dot with the halved olives. Serve the crostini garnished with sprigs of fresh basil.

INGREDIENTS

4 tablespoons olive oil
2 garlic cloves
4 tomatoes, peeled and chopped
1 tablespoon chopped fresh basil
1 tablespoon tomato paste
1 small baguette (large enough to give 8 slices)
8 canned anchovy fillets
12 black olives, halved and pitted
salt and freshly ground black pepper
fresh basil, to garnish

MAKES 8

1 Heat half the olive oil in a frying pan and fry the whole garlic cloves with the chopped tomatoes for about 4 minutes. Stir in the chopped basil and tomato paste and season with plenty of salt and freshly ground black pepper.

Variation

CROSTINI WITH ONION AND OLIVE

Fry 2 large onions, sliced, in 2 tablespoons olive oil until golden. Stir in 8 chopped anchovy fillets, 12 halved, pitted black olives, some seasoning, and 1 teaspoon dried thyme. Spread the bread with 1 tablespoon black olive paste and cover with the onion mixture.

Meat Dishes

Succulent cuts of meat are often the starting point when planning a meal cooked on the grill, and charbroiling gives meat a unique flavor. A perfect steak or lamb chop, simply seasoned and brushed with oil before broiling, is utterly delicious. Even ordinary sausages and burgers for an impromptu family supper can be turned into a treat on the grill. With a little forethought you can add variety and originality to your cooking by marinating the meat for a few hours before you cook it. The simplest marinade will work wonders, improving the texture and juiciness of the meat as well as adding the flavors of herbs and spices. The recipes in this chapter draw on cuisines from all over the world to offer an exciting range of dishes that are all easy to prepare and delicious.

Mixed Grill Skewers with Horseradish Sauce

This hearty selection of meats, cooked on a skewer and drizzled with horseradish sauce, makes a popular main course. Keep all the pieces of meat about the same thickness so they cook evenly.

INGREDIENTS

4 small lamb noisettes, each about 1 inch thick
4 lamb kidneys
4 slices lean bacon
8 cherry tomatoes
8 chipolata sausages
12–16 bay leaves
salt and freshly ground black pepper

FOR THE HORSERADISH SAUCE
2 tablespoons horseradish relish
3 tablespoons melted butter

SERVES 4

1 Trim any excess fat from the lamb noisettes with a sharp knife. Halve the kidneys and remove the cores, using kitchen scissors.

2 Cut each bacon slice in half and wrap around the tomatoes and kidneys.

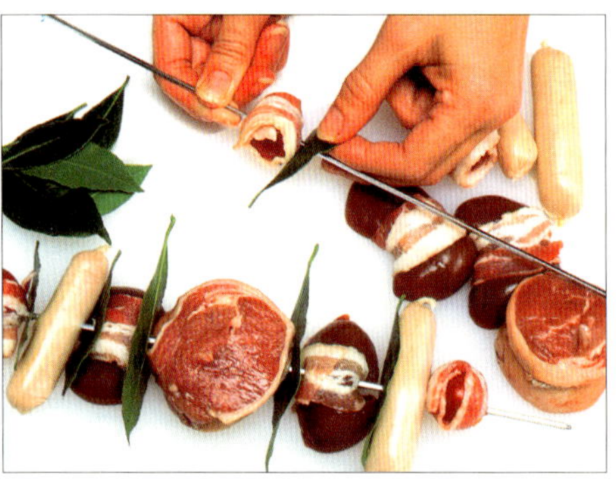

3 Thread the lamb noisettes, bacon-wrapped kidneys and cherry tomatoes, chipolatas and bay leaves onto 4 long metal skewers. Set aside while you prepare the sauce.

4 Mix the horseradish relish with the melted butter in a small bowl and stir until thoroughly mixed.

5 Brush a little of the horseradish sauce over the meat and sprinkle with salt and freshly ground black pepper.

6 Cook the skewers on a medium grill for 12 minutes, turning them occasionally, until the meat is golden brown and thoroughly cooked. Serve hot, drizzled with the remaining sauce.

Sausages with Prunes and Bacon

Sausages are a perennial barbecue favorite, and this is a delicious and unusual way to prepare them. Serve with crusty French bread or warmed ciabatta.

INGREDIENTS

8 large garlic and herb pork sausages, or other good-quality meaty sausages
2 tablespoons Dijon mustard, plus extra to serve
24 pitted prunes
8 slices lean smoked bacon

SERVES 4

1 Use a sharp knife to cut a long slit down the length of each sausage, about three-quarters of the way through.

2 Spread the cut surface with the mustard and then place 3 prunes in each sausage, pressing them in firmly.

3 Stretch the bacon slices out thinly, using the back of a metal spatula.

4 Wrap one bacon slice tightly around each of the sausages, to hold them in shape. Cook over a hot grill for 15–18 minutes, turning occasionally, until evenly browned and thoroughly cooked. Serve at once, with lots of fresh crusty bread and mustard.

SHISH KEBAB

Many different kinds of kebab are eaten throughout the Middle East, and they are almost always cooked over an open wood or charcoal fire.

INGREDIENTS

1 pound boned leg of lamb, cubed
1 large green bell pepper, seeded and cut into squares
1 large yellow bell pepper, seeded and cut into squares
8 baby onions, halved
8 ounces button mushrooms
4 tomatoes, halved
1 tablespoons melted butter
bulgur, to serve

FOR THE MARINADE

3 tablespoons olive oil
juice of 1 lemon
2 garlic cloves, crushed
1 large onion, grated
1 tablespoon fresh oregano
salt and freshly ground black pepper

SERVES 4

1 First make the marinade: Blend together the olive oil, lemon juice, crushed garlic, onion, fresh oregano and seasoning. Place the meat in a shallow dish and pour the marinade over it. Cover with plastic wrap and allow to marinate for several hours, or overnight, in the refrigerator.

2 Thread the lamb onto metal skewers, alternating with pieces of pepper, onions and mushrooms. Thread the tomatoes onto separate skewers.

3 Cook the kebabs and tomatoes on a hot grill for 10 minutes, turning occasionally and basting with butter. Serve with prepared bulgur.

BACON KOFTA KEBABS AND SALAD

Kofta kebabs can be made with any type of ground meat, but bacon is very successful, if you have a food processor.

INGREDIENTS

9 ounces lean bacon slices, roughly chopped
1 small onion, roughly chopped
1 celery stick, roughly chopped
5 tablespoons fresh whole-wheat bread crumbs
3 tablespoons chopped fresh thyme
2 tablespoons Worcestershire sauce
1 egg, beaten
salt and freshly ground black pepper
olive oil, for brushing

FOR THE SALAD

3/4 cup bulgur wheat
4 tablespoons toasted sunflower seeds
1 tablespoon olive oil
salt and freshly ground black pepper
handful of celery leaves, chopped

SERVES 4

1 Place the bacon, onion, celery and bread crumbs in a food processor and process until chopped. Add the thyme, Worcestershire sauce and seasoning. Bind to a firm mixture with the egg.

2 Divide the mixture into 8 equal portions and use your hands to shape them around 8 bamboo skewers.

3 For the salad, place the bulgur in a bowl and pour boiling water over it to cover. Let stand for 30 minutes, until the grains are tender.

4 Drain well, then stir in the sunflower seeds, olive oil, salt and pepper. Stir in the celery leaves.

5 Cook the kofta skewers over a medium-hot grill for 8–10 minutes, turning occasionally, until golden brown. Serve with the salad.

Ham Pizzettas with Melted Brie and Mango

These little individual pizzas are topped with an unusual but very successful combination of smoked ham, Brie and juicy chunks of fresh mango.

INGREDIENTS

2 cups white bread flour
1/4-ounce envelope active dry yeast
2/3 cup warm water
4 tablespoons olive oil

For the topping

1 ripe mango
5 ounces smoked ham, sliced wafer-thin
5 ounces Brie cheese, diced
12 yellow cherry tomatoes, halved
salt and freshly ground black pepper

Serves 6

1 In a large bowl, stir together the flour and yeast, with a pinch of salt. Make a well in the center and stir in the water and 3 tablespoons of the olive oil. Stir until thoroughly mixed.

Cook's Tip

It's important to flatten out the dough rounds quite thinly and to cook them fairly slowly, or they will not cook evenly. To save time, you could use an 11-ounce package of pizza-dough mix.

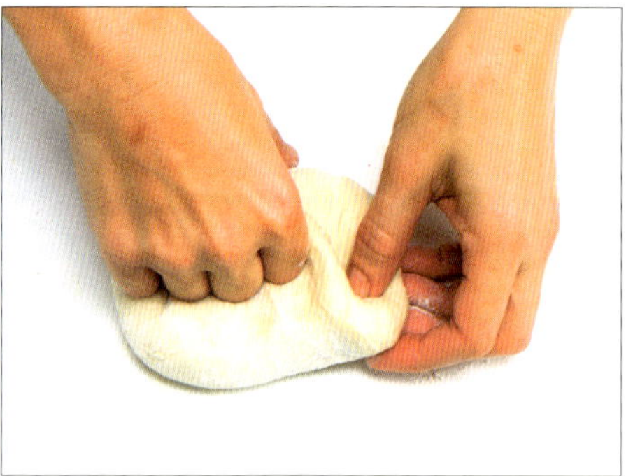

2 Turn the dough out onto a floured surface and knead it for 5 minutes, or until smooth.

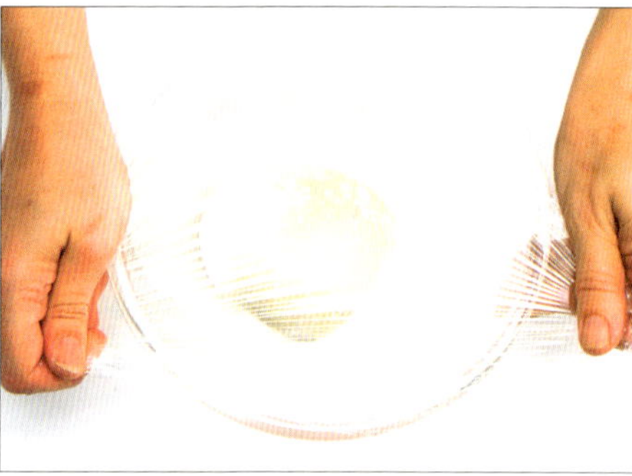

3 Return the dough to the bowl and cover it with a damp cloth or oiled plastic wrap. Set the dough aside in a warm place for about 30 minutes, or until it is doubled in size and springy to the touch.

4 Divide the dough into 6 pieces and roll each piece into a ball. Flatten out with your hand and use your knuckles to press each piece of dough into a round about 6 inches in diameter, with a raised lip around the edge.

5 Halve, pit and peel the mango and cut it into small dice. Arrange with the ham on top of the pizzettas. Top with cheese and tomatoes and sprinkle with salt and ground black pepper.

6 Drizzle the remaining oil over the pizzettas. Place them on a medium-hot grill and cook for 8 minutes, until golden brown and crisp underneath.

Pork and Pineapple Satay

This variation on the classic Thai satay has added pineapple, but keeps the traditional coconut and peanut sauce.

INGREDIENTS

1 1/4 pound pork fillet
1 small onion, chopped
1 garlic clove, chopped
4 tablespoons soy sauce
finely grated rind of 1/2 lemon
1 teaspoon ground cumin
1 teaspoon ground coriander
1 teaspoon ground turmeric
1 teaspoon dark brown sugar
1 8-ounce can pineapple chunks in juice, or 1 small fresh pineapple, peeled and diced
salt and freshly ground black pepper

FOR THE SATAY SAUCE

3/4 cup coconut milk
6 tablespoons crunchy peanut butter
1 garlic clove, crushed
2 teaspoons soy sauce
1 teaspoon dark brown sugar

SERVES 4

1 Using a sharp kitchen knife, trim any fat from the pork fillet and cut it into 1-inch cubes. Place the meat in a large mixing bowl and set aside.

2 Place the onion, garlic, soy sauce, lemon rind, spices and sugar in a blender or food processor. Add two pieces of pineapple and process until the mixture is almost smooth.

3 Add to the pork, tossing well to coat evenly. Thread pork onto bamboo skewers (soak skewers in water first), with the remaining pineapple pieces.

4 To make the sauce, pour the coconut milk into a small saucepan and stir in the peanut butter. Stir in the remaining sauce ingredients and heat gently on the grill, stirring, until smooth and hot. Cover and keep warm on the edge of the grill.

5 Cook the pork and pineapple skewers on a medium-hot grill for 10–12 minutes, turning occasionally, until golden brown and thoroughly cooked. Serve with the satay sauce.

Cook's Tip

You can use creamed coconut, a solid available in blocks at Asian markets, to make the coconut milk. Dissolve a 2-ounce piece in 2/3 cup boiling water and use as above.

OYSTER AND BACON BROCHETTES

Six oysters per person make a good appetizer, served with the seasoned oyster liquor to trickle over the skewers. Alternatively, serve nine per person as a main course, accompanied by a salad.

INGREDIENTS

36 oysters
18 thin-cut slices lean bacon
1 tablespoon paprika
1 teaspoon cayenne pepper
freshly ground black pepper
celery leaves and red chilies, to garnish

FOR THE SAUCE

½ fresh red chili, seeded and very finely chopped
1 garlic clove, crushed
2 scallions, very finely chopped
2 tablespoons finely chopped fresh parsley
liquor from the oysters
juice of ¼–½ lemon, to taste
salt and freshly ground black pepper

SERVES 4–6

1 Open the oysters over a bowl to catch their liquor for the sauce. Wrap your left hand (if you are right-handed) in a clean dish towel and cup the deep shell of each oyster in your wrapped hand. Work the point of a strong, short-bladed knife into the hinge between the shells and twist firmly.

2 Push the knife in and cut the muscle, holding the shell closed. Pour the liquor into the bowl. Cut the oyster free. Discard the drained shells.

3 For the sauce, mix the chili, garlic, scallions and parsley into the oyster liquor and sharpen to taste with lemon juice. Season with salt and pepper and transfer to a serving dish.

4 Cut each bacon slice across the middle. Season the oysters lightly with paprika, cayenne and freshly ground black pepper and wrap each one in half a bacon slice, then thread them onto skewers. Cook on a hot grill for about 5 minutes, turning frequently, until the bacon is crisp and brown. Garnish with celery leaves and red chilies and serve with the sauce.

Lemongrass Pork Chops with Mushrooms

Thai flavorings are used to make an aromatic marinade and a spicy sauce. The sauce can be put together in a pan on the grill while the chops and mushrooms are cooking.

INGREDIENTS

4 pork chops, about 8 ounces each
4 large field mushrooms
3 tablespoons vegetable oil
4 fresh red chilies, seeded and finely sliced
3 tablespoons Thai fish sauce
6 tablespoons lime juice
4 shallots, chopped
1 teaspoon roasted ground rice
2 tablespoons chopped scallions
fresh cilantro leaves, to garnish
4 scallions, shredded, to garnish

FOR THE MARINADE

2 garlic cloves, chopped
1 tablespoon sugar
1 tablespoon Thai fish sauce
2 tablespoons soy sauce
1 tablespoon sesame oil
1 tablespoon whiskey or dry sherry
2 stalks lemongrass, finely chopped
2 scallions, chopped

SERVES 4

1 To make the marinade, mix all the ingredients. Arrange the pork chops in a shallow dish. Pour the marinade over them and let sit for 1–2 hours.

2 Place the mushrooms and marinated pork chops on a rack and brush with 1 tablespoon vegetable oil. On a medium-hot grill, cook the pork chops for 10–15 minutes and the mushrooms for about 2 minutes, turning once. Brush both with the marinade while cooking.

3 Meanwhile, heat the remaining oil in a small frying pan, then remove from the heat and mix in the remaining ingredients. Put the pork chops and mushrooms on a serving plate and spoon the sauce over them. Garnish with the fresh cilantro leaves and shredded scallions.

Peppered Steaks in Beer and Garlic

The robust flavors of this dish will satisfy the heartiest appetites. Serve the steaks with baked potatoes and a crisp mixed salad.

2 Remove the steaks from the dish and reserve the marinade. Sprinkle the peppercorns over the steaks, and press them into the surface.

3 Cook the steaks on a hot grill, basting them occasionally with the reserved marinade during cooking. (Take care when basting, as the alcohol will tend to flare up: Spoon or brush on just a small amount at a time.)

INGREDIENTS

4 beef sirloin or round steaks, about 6 ounces each
2 garlic cloves, crushed
½ cup brown ale or stout
2 tablespoons dark brown sugar
2 tablespoons Worcestershire sauce
1 tablespoon corn oil
1 tablespoon crushed black peppercorns

Serves 4

1 Place the steaks in a dish and add the garlic, ale or stout, sugar, Worcestershire sauce and oil. Turn to coat evenly, then let marinate in the refrigerator for 2–3 hours or overnight.

4 Turn the steaks once during cooking, and cook them for about 3–6 minutes on each side, depending on how rare you like them.

BEEF RIB WITH ONION SAUCE

Rib of beef is a classic large cut for roasting, but just one rib, grilled on the bone, and then carved into succulent slices, makes a perfect dish for two. Serve with a mellow red onion sauce.

INGREDIENTS

1 beef rib on the bone, about 2¼ pounds and about 1½ inches thick, well trimmed of fat
1 teaspoon "steak pepper" or lightly crushed black peppercorns
1 tablespoon coarse sea salt, crushed
2–3 tablespoons olive oil

FOR THE RED ONION SAUCE

3 tablespoons butter
1 large red onion or 8–10 shallots, sliced
1 cup beef or chicken stock
1–2 tablespoons red currant jelly
¼ teaspoon dried thyme
salt and freshly ground black pepper

SERVES 2

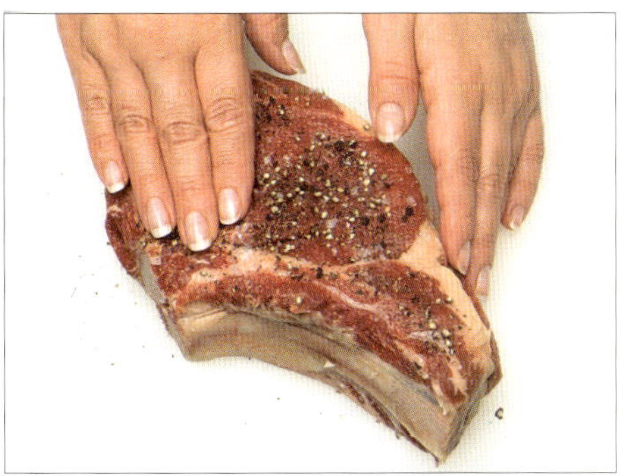

1 Wipe the beef with damp paper towels. Mix the steak pepper or crushed peppercorns with the crushed salt and press onto both sides of the meat. Let the meat stand, loosely covered, for 30 minutes.

2 To make the sauce, melt the butter over medium heat. Add the onion or shallots and cook for 3 minutes, until softened. Add the wine, stock, jelly and thyme and bring to a boil. Reduce the heat and simmer for 30–35 minutes, until the liquid has evaporated and the sauce has thickened. Season and keep warm.

3 Brush the meat with olive oil and cook on a hot grill, or in a pan over high heat, for 5–8 minutes on each side, depending on how rare you like it. Transfer the beef to a board, cover loosely and let stand for about 10 minutes. Using a knife, loosen the meat from the rib bone, then carve into thick slices. Serve with the onion sauce.

STILTON BURGERS

A variation on the traditional hamburger, this tasty recipe contains a delicious surprise: a creamy filling of lightly melted Stilton cheese.

INGREDIENTS

1 pound ground beef
1 onion, chopped
1 celery stick, chopped
1 teaspoon dried mixed herbs
1 teaspoon prepared mustard
½ cup crumbled Stilton cheese
4 hamburger buns
salt and freshly ground black pepper
salad and mustard pickle, to serve

SERVES 4

1 Mix the ground beef with the chopped onion, celery, mixed herbs and mustard. Season well with salt and pepper, and bring together with your hands to form a firm mixture.

2 Divide the mixture into 8 equal portions. Shape 4 portions into rounds and flatten each one slightly. Place a little of the crumbled cheese in the center of each round.

3 Shape and flatten the remaining four portions and place on top. Use your hands to mold the rounds together, encasing the crumbled cheese and shaping them into four burgers.

4 Cook on a medium grill for about 10 minutes or until cooked through, turning once. Split the hamburger buns and place a burger inside each one. Serve with salad and mustard pickle.

Vegetable-Stuffed Beef Rolls

These Japanese-style beef rolls are very popular for al fresco meals. You could roll up many other vegetables in the sliced beef. Pork is also very good cooked this way.

INGREDIENTS

2 ounces carrot
2 ounces green pepper, seeded
1 bunch of scallions
14 ounces beef round, thinly sliced
all-purpose flour, for dusting
1 tablespoon olive oil
fresh parsley sprigs, to garnish

FOR THE SAUCE

2 tablespoons sugar
3 tablespoons soy sauce
3 tablespoons mirin

SERVES 4

1 Use a sharp knife to shred the carrot and green pepper into $1\frac{1}{2}$- to 2-inch lengths. Wash and peel the outer skins from the scallions, then halve them lengthwise. Shred the scallions diagonally into $1\frac{1}{2}$- to 2-inch lengths.

2 The beef slices should be cut paper thin and measure about 6 inches square. Lay a slice of beef on a chopping board and top with strips of the carrot, green pepper and scallion. Roll up tightly and dust lightly with flour. Repeat with the remaining beef and vegetables.

3 Secure the beef rolls with toothpicks, soaked in water to prevent them from burning, and cook on a medium grill, or in a pan over medium heat, for 10–15 minutes, turning frequently, until golden brown and thoroughly cooked.

4 Blend the ingredients for the sauce in a small pan and heat to dissolve the sugar and form a glaze. Halve the cooked rolls, cutting at a slant, and stand them on a plate with the sloping cut ends facing upward. Dress with the sauce and garnish with fresh parsley.

VEAL CHOPS WITH BASIL BUTTER

Veal chops from the loin are an expensive cut and are best cooked quickly and simply. The flavor of basil goes well with veal, but other herbs can be used instead if you prefer.

INGREDIENTS

2 tablespoons butter, softened
1 tablespoon Dijon mustard
1 tablespoon chopped fresh basil
olive oil, for brushing
2 veal loin chops, 1-inch thick, 8 ounces each
salt and freshly ground black pepper
fresh basil sprigs, to garnish

SERVES 2

1 To make the basil butter, cream the softened butter with the Dijon mustard and chopped fresh basil in a large mixing bowl, then season with plenty of freshly ground black pepper.

2 Brush both sides of each chop with olive oil and season with a little salt.

3 Cook the chops on a hot grill for 7–10 minutes, basting with oil and turning once, until done to your liking. (Medium-rare meat will still be slightly soft when pressed, medium meat will be springy, and well-done firm.) Top each chop with half the basil butter and serve at once, garnished with basil.

Skewered Lamb with Cilantro Yogurt

These Turkish kebabs are traditionally made with lamb, but lean beef or pork works equally well. You can alternate pieces of bell pepper, lemon or onions with the meat for extra flavor and color.

INGREDIENTS

2 pounds boneless lean lamb
1 large onion, grated
3 bay leaves
5 sprigs of thyme or rosemary
grated rind and juice of 1 lemon
½ teaspoon sugar
⅓ cup olive oil
salt and freshly ground black pepper
sprigs of fresh rosemary, to garnish
barbecued lemon wedges, to serve

FOR THE CILANTRO YOGURT

⅔ cup thick plain yogurt
1 tablespoon chopped fresh mint
1 tablespoon chopped fresh cilantro
2 teaspoons grated onion

SERVES 4

1 To make the cilantro yogurt, mix together the yogurt, mint, cilantro and grated onion. Transfer the yogurt to a serving bowl or cover and store in the refridgerator until ready to serve.

2 To make the kebabs, cut the lamb into 1-inch cubes and place in a bowl. Mix together the onion, herbs, lemon rind and juice, sugar and oil, then season to taste.

3 Pour the marinade over the meat in the bowl and stir so that the meat is thoroughly covered. Cover with plastic wrap and marinate in the refrigerator for several hours or overnight.

4 Drain the meat and thread onto metal skewers. Cook on a hot grill for about 10 minutes. Garnish with rosemary and grilled lemon wedges and serve with the cilantro yogurt.

Lamb Burgers with Red Currant Chutney

These very special burgers take a little extra time to prepare but are well worth it. The red currant chutney is the perfect complement to the minty lamb taste.

INGREDIENTS

1¼ pounds ground lean lamb
1 small onion, finely chopped
2 tablespoons finely chopped fresh mint
2 tablespoons finely chopped fresh parsley
4 ounces mozzarella cheese
2 tablespoons oil, for basting
salt and freshly ground black pepper

FOR THE RED CURRANT CHUTNEY

1½ cups fresh or frozen red currants
2 teaspoons clear honey
1 teaspoon balsamic vinegar
2 tablespoons finely chopped mint

SERVES 4

1 In a large bowl, mix together the ground lamb, chopped onion, mint and parsley until evenly combined. Season well with plenty of salt and freshly ground black pepper.

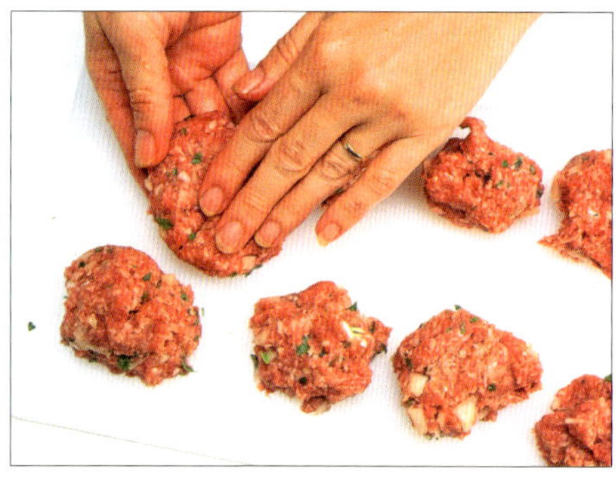

2 Roughly divide the meat mixture into eight equal pieces and use your hands to press each of the pieces into a flat round.

3 Cut the mozzarella into 4 chunks. Place 1 chunk of cheese on half the lamb rounds. Top each one with another round of meat mixture.

4 Press each of the 2 rounds of meat together firmly, making 4 flattish burger shapes. Use your fingers to blend the edges and seal in the cheese completely.

5 Place all the ingredients for the chutney in a bowl and mash them together with a fork. Season well with salt and freshly ground black pepper.

6 Brush the lamb burgers with olive oil and cook them on a moderately hot grill for about 15 minutes, turning once, until golden brown. Serve on hamburger buns with the chutney.

Cook's Tip

If time is short, or if fresh red currants are not available, serve the burgers with ready-made red currant sauce.

Grilled Lamb with Potato Slices

A traditional mixture of fresh herbs adds a summery flavor to this simple lamb dish. The leg of lamb will cook more evenly on the grill if it's boned, or "butterflied," first.

INGREDIENTS

1 leg of lamb, about 4½ pounds
1 garlic clove, thinly sliced
handful of fresh flat-leaf parsley
handful of fresh sage
handful of fresh rosemary
handful of fresh thyme
6 tablespoons dry sherry
4 tablespoons walnut oil
1¼ pounds medium-size potatoes
salt and freshly ground black pepper

SERVES 4

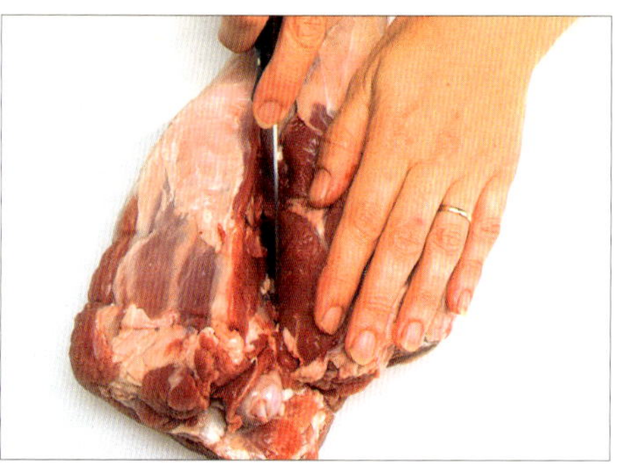

1 Place the lamb on a board, smooth side down, so that you can see where the bone lies. Using a sharp, heavy knife, make a long cut through the flesh down to the bone.

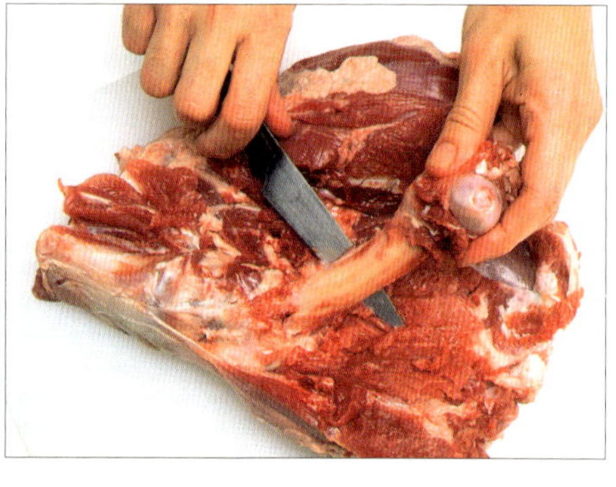

2 Use a sharp kitchen knife to scrape away the meat from the bone on both sides, until the bone is completely exposed. Carefully remove the bone and cut away any sinews and excess fat from the meat.

3 Cut through the thickest part of the meat so that you can open it out as flat as possible. (Your butcher can butterfly the meat for you if you prefer.) Then make several cuts in the lamb with a sharp kitchen knife, and push slivers of garlic and sprigs of fresh herbs into the cuts.

4 Place the meat in a bowl and pour the sherry and walnut oil over it. Chop half the remaining herbs and sprinkle over the meat. Cover the bowl with a clean dish towel and let marinate in the refrigerator for 30 minutes.

5 Remove the lamb from the marinade and season it. Cook on a medium-hot grill for 30–35 minutes, turning occasionally and basting with the reserved marinade.

6 Scrub the potatoes, then slice them thickly. Brush with the marinade and place around the lamb. Cook for about 15 minutes, until golden brown.

Cook's Tip

If you have a spit-roasting attachment, the lamb can be rolled and tied with herbs inside, and spit roasted for 1–1½ hours. A spit makes it much easier to cook larger pieces of lamb.

LAMB WITH LAVENDER BALSAMIC MARINADE

Lavender is an unusual flavor to use with meat, but its heady, summery scent works well with grilled lamb. If you prefer, rosemary can take its place.

INGREDIENTS

4 racks of lamb, with 3–4 cutlets each
1 shallot, finely chopped
3 tablespoons chopped fresh lavender
1 tablespoon balsamic vinegar
2 tablespoons olive oil
1 tablespoon lemon juice
salt and freshly ground black pepper
handful of lavender sprigs

SERVES 4

1 Place the racks of lamb in a large mixing bowl or wide dish and sprinkle the chopped shallot over them.

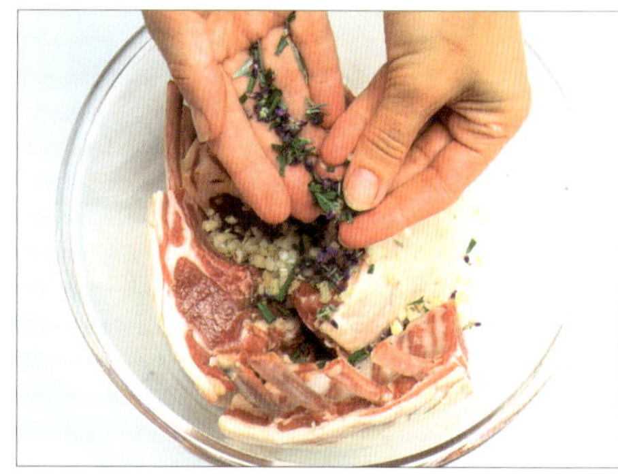

2 Sprinkle the chopped fresh lavender over the lamb in the bowl.

3 Beat together the vinegar, olive oil and lemon juice and pour over the lamb. Season well with salt and pepper, then turn to coat evenly.

4 Sprinkle a few lavender sprigs over the broiler or on the coals of a medium-hot grill. Cook the lamb for 15–20 minutes, turning once and basting with any remaining marinade, until golden brown on the outside and still slightly pink in the center.

Lamb with Mint and Lemon

Use this simple and traditional marinade to make the most of fine-quality lamb leg steaks. Lemon and fresh mint combine extremely well with the flavor of grilled lamb.

INGREDIENTS

4 lamb steaks, about 8 ounces each
fresh mint leaves, to garnish

FOR THE MARINADE

grated rind and juice of ½ lemon
1 garlic clove, crushed
1 scallion, finely chopped
1 teaspoon finely chopped fresh mint
2 tablespoons extra virgin olive oil
salt and freshly ground black pepper

SERVES 4

1 Mix all the marinade ingredients and season to taste. Place the lamb steaks in a shallow dish and add the marinade. Cover with plastic wrap and allow to marinate in the refrigerator for several hours or overnight.

2 Drain the lamb from the marinade and cook on a medium-hot grill for 10–15 minutes or until just cooked, basting occasionally with the marinade and turning once. Garnish the lamb steaks with the fresh mint leaves.

JUNIPER-SPICED VENISON CHOPS

Depending on the type of venison available, the chops will vary in size, so you will need either one or two per person.

INGREDIENTS

4–8 venison chops
1 cup red wine
2 medium red onions
6 juniper berries, crushed
1 cinnamon stick, crumbled
1 dried bay leaf, crumbled
thinly pared strip of orange rind
olive oil, for brushing
salt and freshly ground black pepper

SERVES 4

2 Add the juniper berries, cinnamon, bay leaf and orange rind. Toss well to coat evenly and then cover the bowl and allow to marinate for at least an hour, or overnight in the refrigerator.

1 Place the venison chops in a large mixing bowl and pour the red wine over them. Using a sharp knife, cut the red onions in half crosswise and add them to the bowl.

3 Drain the venison and onions and reserve the marinade. Brush the venison and onions generously with the olive oil and sprinkle with plenty of salt and freshly ground black pepper.

4 Cook the venison and onions on a medium-hot grill for 8–10 minutes on each side, turning once and basting regularly with the marinade. The venison should still be slightly pink inside even when fully cooked.

Cook's Tip

Tender farmed venison is now widely available from supermarkets and good butcher shops, but if you can't find it, beef steaks could be used instead.

Poultry and Game

Chicken cooked on the grill is unfailingly popular with both adults and children, and it can be as simple or sophisticated as you choose: it is very versatile and takes on a whole range of flavors with great success. Buy breast fillets to make delicious kebabs and salads with a minimum of preparation, or cook drumsticks and thighs with robust spicy coatings. Whole birds can be roasted very effectively on a spit, or they can be flattened out by removing the backbone and cooked on the grill rack. It is vital to make sure chicken is always very thoroughly cooked – it needs a medium heat to cook it through without charring the outside. Don't forget other types of poultry, particularly duck, which stays beautifully juicy and moist when cooked on the grill.

CHICKEN WITH PINEAPPLE

The pineapple juice in this Indian recipe is used to tenderize the meat, but it also gives the chicken a deliciously tangy sweetness.

INGREDIENTS

18-ounce can pineapple chunks in juice
1 teaspoon ground cumin
1 teaspoon ground coriander
1 garlic clove, crushed
1 teaspoon chili powder
1 teaspoon salt
2 tablespoons low-fat plain yogurt
1 tablespoon chopped fresh cilantro
few drops orange food coloring (optional)
10 ounces skinned, boned chicken breast and thigh meat, about 2 cups
½ red bell pepper
½ yellow or green bell pepper
1 large onion
6 cherry tomatoes
1 tablespoon vegetable oil
salad or rice, to serve

SERVES 6

1 Drain the canned pineapple into a bowl. Reserve 12 large chunks of pineapple. Squeeze the juice from the remaining chunks into the bowl, then discard the chunks. You should be left with about ½ cup pineapple juice.

2 In a large bowl, blend together the cumin, ground coriander, garlic, chili powder, salt, yogurt, fresh cilantro and food coloring, if using. Pour in the pineapple juice and mix together.

3 Cut the chicken into cubes, add to the yogurt and spice mixture and set aside to marinate for 1–1½ hours. Cut the peppers and onion into chunks.

4 Arrange the chicken pieces, vegetables and reserved pineapple chunks alternately on 6 skewers.

5 Brush the kebabs with oil and cook on a medium grill for about 10 minutes, turning regularly and basting the chicken pieces regularly with the marinade, until cooked through. Serve with salad or plain cooked rice.

CITRUS KEBABS

Serve these succulent grilled chicken kebabs on a bed of lettuce leaves, garnished with sprigs of fresh mint and orange and lemon slices.

INGREDIENTS

4 chicken breasts, skinned and boned
fresh mint sprigs, to garnish
orange, lemon or lime slices, to garnish

FOR THE MARINADE

finely grated rind and juice of ½ orange
finely grated rind and juice of ½ lemon or lime
2 tablespoons olive oil
2 tablespoons clear honey
2 tablespoons chopped fresh mint
¼ teaspoon ground cumin
salt and freshly ground black pepper

SERVES 4

1 Use a heavy knife to cut the chicken into 1-inch cubes.

2 Mix the marinade ingredients together in a large mixing bowl, add the chicken and cover with plastic wrap. Allow to marinate for at least 2 hours, or overnight in the refrigerator.

3 Thread the chicken onto metal skewers and cook on a medium grill for 10 minutes, basting with the marinade and turning frequently. Garnish with mint and citrus slices.

SWEET AND SOUR KEBABS

This marinade contains sugar and will burn very easily, so cook the kebabs slowly and turn them often. Serve these kebabs with Harlequin Rice.

INGREDIENTS

2 chicken breasts, skinned and boned
8 pearl onions or 2 medium onions
4 slices lean bacon
3 firm bananas
1 red bell pepper, diced

FOR THE MARINADE
2 tablespoons brown sugar
1 tablespoon Worcestershire sauce
2 tablespoons lemon juice
salt and freshly ground black pepper

FOR THE HARLEQUIN RICE
2 tablespoons olive oil
1 small red bell pepper, diced
generous 1 cup cooked rice
1 cup cooked peas

SERVES 4

1 Mix together the marinade ingredients. Cut each chicken breast into four pieces, add to the marinade, cover and leave for at least 4 hours, or preferably overnight in the refrigerator.

2 Peel the pearl onions, blanch them in boiling water for 5 minutes and drain. If using medium onions, quarter them after blanching.

3 Cut each slice of bacon in half with a sharp knife. Peel the bananas and cut each one into three pieces. Wrap half a bacon rasher around each of the banana pieces.

4 Thread the bacon and bananas onto metal skewers with the chicken pieces, onions and pepper pieces. Brush generously with the marinade.

5 Cook on a low grill for about 15 minutes, turning and basting frequently with the marinade.

6 Meanwhile, heat the oil in a frying pan and stir-fry the diced pepper briefly. Add the rice and peas and stir until heated through. Serve Harlequin Rice with the kebabs.

BLACKENED CAJUN CHICKEN AND CORN

This is a classic Deep South method of cooking in a spiced coating, which can be used for poultry, meat or fish. The coating should begin to char and blacken slightly at the edges.

INGREDIENTS

8 chicken joints (drumsticks, thighs or wings)
2 ears of fresh corn
2 teaspoons garlic salt
2 teaspoons ground black pepper
1½ teaspoons ground cumin
1½ teaspoons paprika
1 teaspoon cayenne pepper
3 tablespoons melted butter
chopped parsley, to garnish

SERVES 4

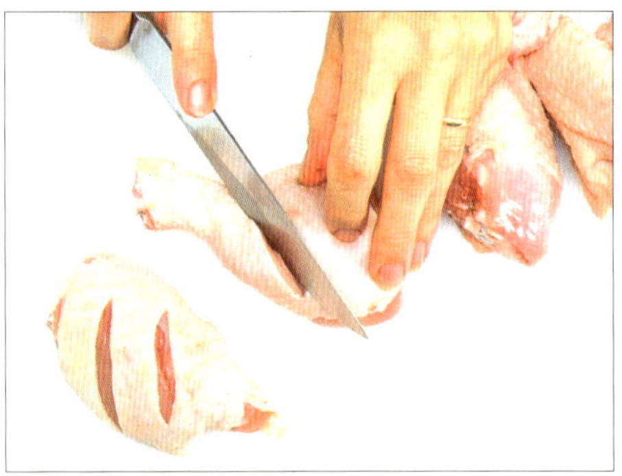

1 Trim any excess fat from the chicken, but leave the skin in place. Slash the thickest parts with a knife, to allow the flavors to penetrate the meat as much as possible.

2 Pull the husks and silks off the ears of corn, then rinse them under cold running water and pat them dry with paper towels. Cut into thick slices, using a heavy kitchen knife.

3 Mix together all the spices. Brush the chicken and corn with the melted butter and sprinkle the spices over them. Toss well to coat evenly.

4 Cook the chicken pieces on a medium-hot grill for about 25 minutes, turning occasionally. Add the corn after 15 minutes and grill, turning often, until golden brown. Serve garnished with chopped parsley.

Chicken with Herb and Ricotta Stuffing

These little chicken drumsticks are full of flavor, and the stuffing and bacon help to keep them moist and tender.

INGREDIENTS

4 tablespoons ricotta cheese
1 garlic clove, crushed
3 tablespoons mixed chopped fresh herbs, such as chives, flat-leaf parsley and mint
2 tablespoons fresh brown bread crumbs
8 chicken drumsticks
8 slices lean smoked bacon
1 teaspoon whole-grain mustard
1 tablespoon sunflower oil
salt and freshly ground black pepper

SERVES 4

1 Mix together the ricotta, garlic, herbs and bread crumbs. Season well with plenty of salt and pepper.

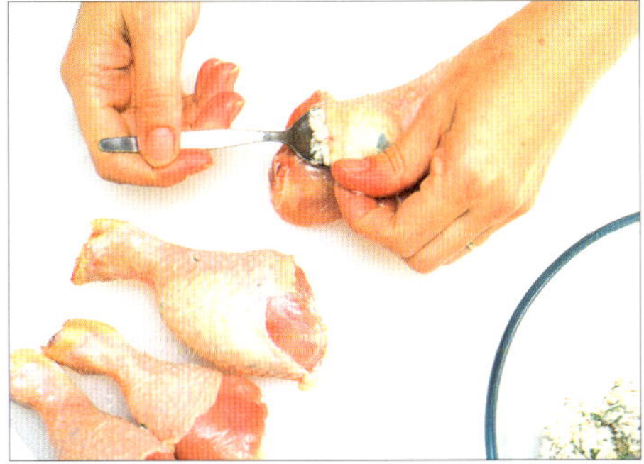

2 Carefully loosen the skin from each drumstick and spoon a little of the herb stuffing underneath, smoothing the skin back over firmly.

3 Wrap a bacon slice tightly around the wide end of each drumstick, to hold the skin in place over the stuffing during cooking.

4 Mix together the mustard and oil and brush them over the chicken. Cook on a medium-hot grill for about 25 minutes, turning occasionally.

Baby Chickens with Lime and Chili

Poussins are small birds that are ideal for one to two portions. The best way to prepare them is spatchcocked—split and flattened out—to ensure more even cooking.

INGREDIENTS

4 poussins or Cornish game hens, about 1 pound each
3 tablespoons butter
2 tablespoons sun-dried tomato paste
finely grated rind of 1 lime
2 teaspoons chili sauce
juice of 1/2 lime
lime wedges, to serve
fresh flat leaf parsley sprigs, to garnish

SERVES 4

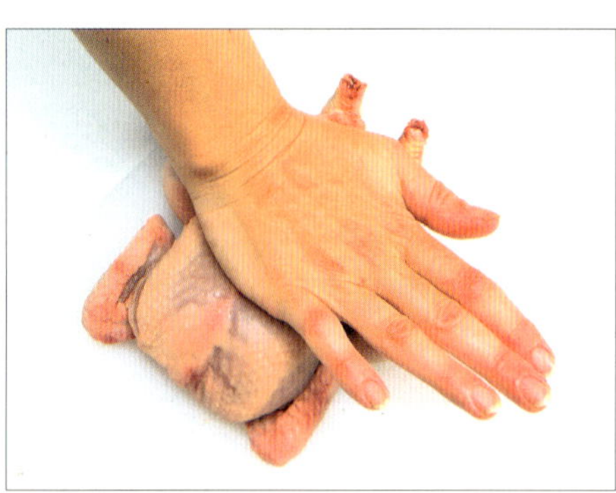

1 Place each poussin or hen on a chopping board, breast side upward, and press down firmly with your hand, to break the breastbone.

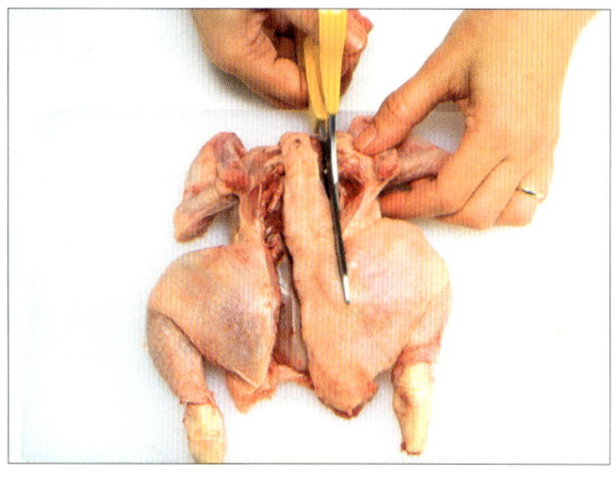

2 Turn the poussin over and, with poultry shears or strong kitchen scissors, cut down either side of the backbone. Remove it and discard.

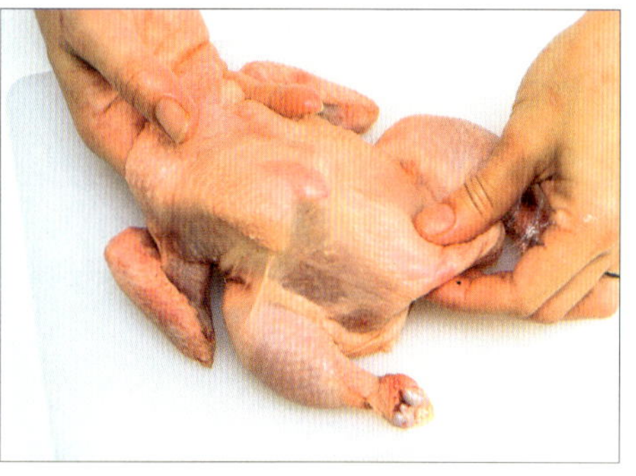

3 Turn the poussin breast side up and flatten it gently. Lift the breast skin carefully and gently ease your fingertips underneath, to loosen it from the flesh.

4 Mix together the butter, sun-dried tomato paste, lime rind and chili sauce in a small bowl. Spread about three-quarters of the mixture under the skin of the poussins, smoothing it evenly over the surface of the flesh.

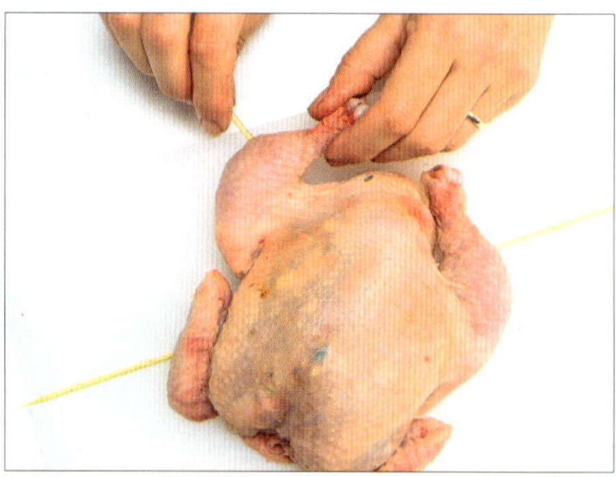

5 To hold the poussins flat during cooking, thread two skewers through each bird, crossing at the center. Each skewer should pass through a drumstick and then out through a wing on the other side.

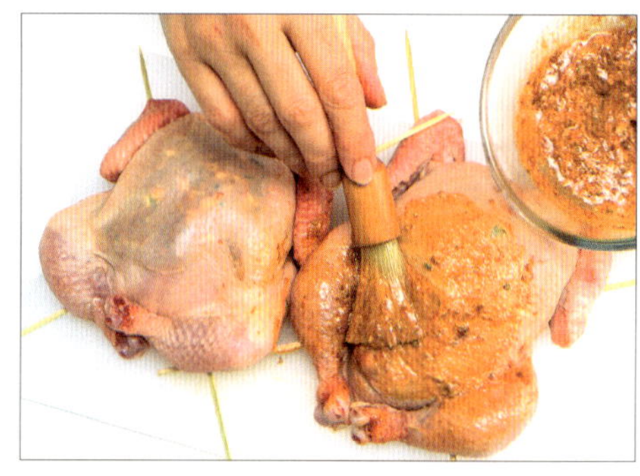

6 Mix the reserved paste with the lime juice and brush it over the skin of the poussins. Cook on a medium-hot grill, turning occasionally, for 25–30 minutes, or until there is no trace of pink in the juices when the flesh is pierced. Garnish with lime wedges and fresh flat leaf parsley.

CHICKEN SALAD WITH CILANTRO DRESSING

Serve this salad warm to make the most of the wonderful flavor of grilled chicken basted with a marinade of coriander, sesame and mustard.

INGREDIENTS

4 medium chicken breasts, skinned and boned
8 ounces snow peas
2 heads decorative lettuce such as lollo rosso or oak leaf
3 carrots, cut into matchsticks
6 ounces button mushrooms, sliced
6 slices bacon, fried and chopped

FOR THE CILANTRO DRESSING
1/2 cup lemon juice
2 tablespoons whole-grain mustard
1 cup olive oil
1/3 cup sesame oil
1 teaspoon coriander seeds, crushed
1 tablespoon chopped fresh cilantro, to garnish

SERVES 6

1 Mix all the dressing ingredients in a bowl. Place the chicken breasts in a dish and pour half the dressing over them. Marinate overnight in the refrigerator; refrigerate the remaining dressing.

2 Cook the snow peas in boiling water for 2 minutes, then refresh in cold water. Tear the lettuces into small pieces and mix all the other salad ingredients and the bacon together. Arrange the salad in individual bowls.

3 Cook the chicken breasts on a medium grill for 10–15 minutes, basting with the marinade and turning once, until cooked through. Slice them on the diagonal into thin pieces. Divide among the bowls of salad and add some dressing to each dish. Combine quickly and sprinkle some fresh cilantro over each bowl.

Hot and Sour Chicken Salad

This chicken salad from Vietnam is equally delicious made with shrimp. Allow one pound of fresh shrimp tails to serve four people.

INGREDIENTS

2 chicken breasts, skinned and boned
4 ounces bean sprouts
1 head Chinese cabbage, shredded
2 medium carrots, cut into matchsticks
1 red onion, thinly sliced
2 large gherkins, sliced

FOR THE MARINADE

1 small red chili, seeded and finely chopped
½-in piece fresh ginger, chopped
1 garlic clove, crushed
1 tablespoon crunchy peanut butter
2 tablespoons chopped fresh cilantro
1 teaspoon sugar
½ teaspoon salt
1 tablespoon rice or white wine vinegar
4 tablespoons vegetable oil
2 teaspoons Thai fish sauce

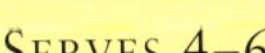

SERVES 4–6

1 Slice the chicken breasts thinly and place in a shallow bowl. Grind the chili, ginger and garlic in a food processor (or grind using a mortar and pestle), then add the peanut butter, chopped fresh cilantro, sugar and salt.

2 Add the rice or white wine vinegar, 2 tablespoons of the oil and the fish sauce to the ingredients in the food processor. Combine well. Cover the chicken with the spice mixture and let it marinate for at least 2–3 hours.

3 Cook the chicken on a medium-hot grill or in a frying pan on the stove for about 5 minutes, basting often and turning once. Arrange the salad ingredients on a serving dish and top with the cooked chicken.

Chicken, Mushroom and Cilantro Pizza

Shiitake mushrooms add an earthy flavor to this colorful pizza, while fresh chili and chili-flavored olive oil give it a hint of spiciness. Cook the pizza on the grill or in the oven.

INGREDIENTS

3 tablespoons olive oil
12 ounces skinned chicken breast fillets, cut into thin strips
1 bunch scallions, sliced
1 fresh red chili, seeded and chopped
1 red bell pepper, cut into thin strips
3 ounces fresh shiitake mushrooms, sliced
3–4 tablespoons chopped fresh cilantro
1 round of pizza dough, 10–12 inches in diameter
1 tablespoon chili oil
5 ounces mozzarella cheese
salt and freshly ground black pepper

Serves 3–4

1 Heat 2 tablespoons olive oil in a wok or large frying pan. Add the chicken, scallions, chili, red pepper and mushrooms and stir-fry over high heat for 2–3 minutes, until the chicken is firm but still slightly pink inside. Season to taste.

2 Pour off any excess oil, then set aside to let the chicken mixture cool.

3 Stir the fresh cilantro into the cooled chicken mixture in the wok.

4 Brush all over the top of the pizza-dough round with the chili oil.

5 Spoon on the chicken mixture and drizzle with the remaining olive oil.

6 Grate the mozzarella and sprinkle it over the pizza. Cook the pizza on a medium-hot grill for about 15–20 minutes, until the crust is crisp and golden and the cheese is bubbling. Serve the pizza immediately.

Chicken Cooked in Spices and Coconut

This chicken dish can be prepared in advance until you are ready to light the grill. Serve it with naan (a flat, leavened Indian bread). Creamed coconut can be found in Asian markets.

INGREDIENTS

7-ounce block creamed coconut
1 1/4 cups boiling water
3 garlic cloves, chopped
2 scallions, chopped
1 fresh green chili, chopped
2-inch piece fresh ginger, chopped
1 teaspoon fennel seeds
1/2 teaspoon black peppercorns
seeds from 4 cardamom pods
2 tablespoons ground coriander
1 teaspoon ground cumin
1 teaspoon ground star anise
1 teaspoon ground nutmeg
1/2 teaspoon ground cloves
1/2 teaspoon ground turmeric
4 large chicken breasts, skinned and boned
onion rings and fresh cilantro sprigs, to garnish

SERVES 4

1 Break up the coconut and put it in a bowl. Pour the boiling water over it and set aside to dissolve. Place the chopped garlic, scallions, chili, ginger and all of the spices in a blender or food processor. Pour in the coconut mixture and blend to a smooth paste.

2 Make several diagonal cuts across the chicken breasts. Arrange in a layer in a shallow dish. Spoon on half the coconut mixture and toss well to coat evenly. Cover the dish and let the chicken marinate for at least 30 minutes, or overnight in the refrigerator.

3 Cook the chicken on a medium grill for 12–15 minutes, turning once, until well browned and thoroughly cooked. Heat the remaining coconut mixture gently until boiling. Serve with the chicken, garnished with onion rings and sprigs of cilantro.

Mediterranean Turkey Skewers

These attractive kebabs can be assembled in advance and left to marinate until you are ready to cook them. Grilling intensifies the Mediterranean flavors of the vegetables.

INGREDIENTS

2 medium zucchini
1 long thin eggplant
11 ounces boneless turkey, cut into 2-inch cubes
12–16 pearl onions
1 red or yellow bell pepper, cut into 2-inch squares

FOR THE MARINADE

6 tablespoons olive oil
3 tablespoons fresh lemon juice
1 garlic clove, finely chopped
2 tablespoons chopped fresh basil
salt and freshly ground black pepper

SERVES 4

1 To make the marinade, mix the olive oil with the lemon juice, garlic and chopped fresh basil. Season well with plenty of salt and black pepper.

2 Slice the zucchini and eggplant lengthwise into strips 1/4 inch thick. Cut them crosswise about two-thirds down their length. Discard the shorter lengths. Wrap half the turkey pieces with the zucchini slices and the other half with the eggplant slices.

3 Prepare the skewers by alternating the turkey, onions and pepper pieces. Lay the prepared skewers on a platter and sprinkle with the flavored oil. Allow to marinate for 30 minutes.

4 Cook on a medium grill or under a broiler, turning the skewers occasionally, for about 10 minutes, or until the turkey is cooked and the vegetables are tender.

DUCK BREASTS WITH RED PEPPER JELLY GLAZE

Sweet potatoes have pinkish skins and flesh varying from creamy white to deep orange. Choose a long, cylindrical tuber to make neat round slices for this Cajun dish.

INGREDIENTS

2 duck breasts
1 sweet potato, about 14 ounces
2 tablespoons red pepper jelly
1 tablespoon sherry vinegar
4 tablespoons butter, melted
coarse sea salt and freshly ground black pepper

SERVES 2

1 Slash the skin of the duck breasts diagonally at 1-inch intervals and rub plenty of salt and pepper over the skin and into the cuts.

2 Scrub the sweet potato and cut into ½-inch slices, discarding the ends.

3 Cook the duck breasts on a medium grill, skin side down, for 5 minutes. Turn and cook for another 8–10 minutes, according to how pink you like your duck.

4 Meanwhile, warm the red pepper jelly and sherry vinegar together in a bowl set over a saucepan of hot water, stirring to mix them as the jelly melts. Brush the skin of the duck with this jelly glaze and return to the grill, skin side down, for another 2–3 minutes to caramelize it.

5 Brush the sweet potato slices with melted butter and sprinkle with coarse sea salt. Cook on a hot grill for 8–10 minutes, until soft, brushing with more butter and sprinkling with salt and pepper when you turn them. Serve the duck sliced with the sweet potatoes and accompany with a green salad.

DUCK BREASTS WITH RED PLUMS

The rich fruity sauce for this dish combines brandy and red plums with heavy cream and cilantro. The sauce can be made in a pan on the grill while the duck is cooking.

INGREDIENTS

4 duck breasts, about 6 ounces each, skinned
2 teaspoons crushed cinnamon stick
4 tablespoons butter
1 tablespoon plum brandy or cognac
1 cup chicken stock
1 cup heavy cream
6 fresh red plums, pitted and sliced
6 sprigs fresh cilantro leaves, plus extra to garnish
salt and freshly ground black pepper

SERVES 4

1 Score the duck breasts and sprinkle with salt. Press the crushed cinnamon onto both sides of the duck breasts. Brush with butter and cook on a medium grill for 15–20 minutes, turning once, until the duck is tender.

2 To make the sauce, melt half the remaining butter in a saucepan. Add the brandy or cognac and set it alight. When the flames have died down, add the stock and cream and allow to simmer gently until reduced and thickened. Add seasoning to taste.

3 In a saucepan, melt the other half of the butter and fry the plums with the cilantro just enough to cook the fruit through. Slice the duck breasts and pour some sauce around each one, then garnish with the plum slices and the chopped fresh cilantro.

PHEASANT WITH SAGE AND LEMON

Pheasant is quick to cook and makes a very special summer meal. This recipe can also be used for guinea fowl.

INGREDIENTS

2 pheasant, about 1 pound each
1 lemon
4 tablespoons chopped fresh sage
3 shallots
1 teaspoon Dijon mustard
1 tablespoon brandy or dry sherry
1⅔ cup crème fraîche
salt and freshly ground black pepper
lemon wedges and sage sprigs, to garnish

SERVES 4

1 Place the pheasant, breast side up, on a chopping board and cut them in half lengthwise, using poultry shears or a sharp kitchen knife.

2 Finely grate the rind from half the lemon and slice the rest thinly. Mix together the lemon rind and half the chopped sage in a small bowl.

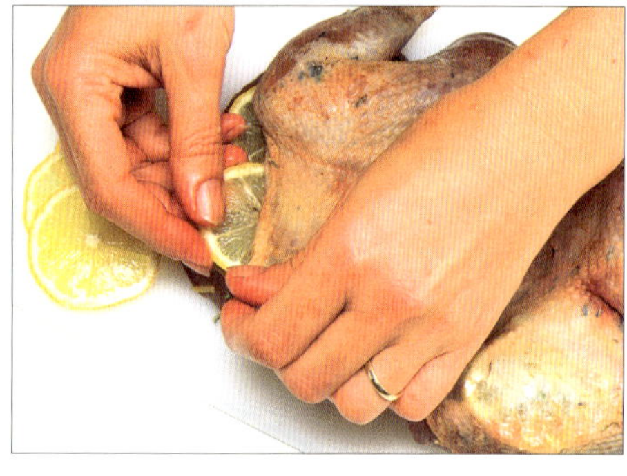

3 Loosen the skin on the breasts and legs of the pheasant and push a little of the sage mixture underneath. Tuck the lemon slices under the skin, smoothing the skin back firmly.

4 Place the half pheasants on a medium-hot grill and cook for 25–30 minutes, turning once.

5 Meanwhile, cook the shallots on the grill for 10–12 minutes, turning occasionally, until the skin is blackened and the inside very soft. Peel off the skins, chop the flesh roughly and mash it with the Dijon mustard and brandy or sherry.

6 Stir in the crème fraîche and add the reserved chopped sage. Season with plenty of salt and freshly ground black pepper. Serve the dressing with the pheasant, garnished with lemon wedges and sprigs of fresh sage.

Cook's Tip

Try to choose pheasant with undamaged skins, so that the flavorings stay in place during cooking.

QUAIL WITH A FIVE-SPICE MARINADE

Blending and grinding your own five-spice powder for this Vietnamese dish will give the freshest-tasting results. If you are short of time, buy a ready-mixed blend from the supermarket.

INGREDIENTS

6 quail, cleaned
2 scallions, roughly chopped, to garnish
mandarin orange or satsuma, to garnish
banana leaves, to serve

FOR THE MARINADE

2 pieces star anise
2 teaspoons ground cinnamon
2 teaspoons fennel seeds
2 teaspoons Sichuan pepper
a pinch ground cloves
1 small onion, finely chopped
1 garlic clove, crushed
4 tablespoons clear honey
2 tablespoons dark soy sauce

SERVES 4–6

1 Remove the backbones from the quail by cutting down each side with a pair of strong kitchen scissors.

2 Flatten the birds with the palm of your hand and secure each bird using two bamboo skewers.

3 To make the marinade, place the five spices in a spice mill and grind into a fine powder (or grind using a mortar and pestle). Add the chopped onion, garlic, clear honey and soy sauce, and combine until thoroughly mixed.

4 Arrange the quail on a flat dish and pour the marinade over them. Cover the dish with plastic wrap and let the quail marinate in the refrigerator for 8 hours or overnight.

5 Cook the quail on a medium grill for 15–20 minutes, until golden brown, basting occasionally with the marinade and turning once.

6 To garnish, remove the outer zest from the mandarin orange or satsuma, using a vegetable peeler. Shred the zest finely and combine with the chopped scallions. Arrange the quail on a bed of banana leaves and garnish with the orange zest and scallions.

Cook's Tip

If you prefer, or if quail are not available, you could use other poultry, such as poussins or Cornish game hens, as a substitute.

Fish and Seafood

Cooking over charcoal adds a marvelous flavor to fish and seafood, and it's very quick and easy to prepare this way. Oily fish such as mackerel or sardines are perfectly suited to broiling and won't dry out, while charbroiling will enhance their robust flavors. Use plump shrimps or meaty-textured fish such as monkfish for kebabs, but marinate them first to keep them moist. More delicate fish, or those that are best cooked in their own steam, can also be grilled successfully: just wrap them securely in aluminum foil and cook them either on the rack or directly on the coals. You can include all kinds of flavorings in the foil parcels, too.

JUMBO SHRIMP SKEWERS WITH WALNUT PESTO

This is an unusual appetizer or main course, which can be prepared in advance and kept in the refrigerator until you're ready to cook it.

INGREDIENTS

12–16 raw, unshelled jumbo shrimp
½ cup walnut pieces
4 tablespoons chopped fresh flat-leaf parsley
4 tablespoons chopped fresh basil
2 garlic cloves, chopped
3 tablespoons grated fresh Parmesan cheese
2 tablespoons extra virgin olive oil
2 tablespoons walnut oil
salt and freshly ground black pepper

SERVES 4

1 Peel the shrimp, removing the heads but leaving the tails. Devein and then put the shrimp in a large mixing bowl.

2 To make the pesto, place the walnuts, parsley, basil, garlic, cheese and oils in a food processor and process until finely chopped. Season.

3 Add half the pesto to the shrimp in the bowl, toss them well, then cover and chill in the refrigerator for a minimum of 1 hour, or overnight.

4 Thread the shrimp onto skewers and cook them on a hot grill for 3–4 minutes, turning once. Serve with the remaining pesto and a green salad.

SPICED SHRIMP WITH VEGETABLES

This is a light and nutritious Indian dish, excellent served either on a bed of lettuce leaves, or with plain boiled rice or chapatis (flat rounds of unleavened bread, available in Asian markets).

INGREDIENTS

20 cooked jumbo shrimp, peeled
1 medium zucchini, thickly sliced
1 medium onion, cut into 8 chunks
8 cherry tomatoes
8 ears of baby corn
mixed salad leaves, to serve

FOR THE MARINADE

2 tablespoons chopped fresh cilantro
1 teaspoon salt
2 fresh green chilies, seeded if desired
3 tablespoons lemon juice
2 tablespoons vegetable oil

SERVES 4

1 To make the marinade, blend the cilantro, salt, chilies, lemon juice and oil together in a food processor.

2 Transfer the contents of the food processor to a bowl.

3 Add the peeled shrimp to the mixture in the bowl and stir to make sure that all the shrimp are well coated. Cover the bowl with plastic wrap and set aside in a cool place to marinate for about 30 minutes.

4 Arrange the vegetables and shrimp alternately on 4 long skewers. Cook on a medium grill for 5 minutes, turning frequently, until cooked and browned. Serve immediately, on a bed of mixed salad leaves.

CALAMARI WITH TWO-TOMATO STUFFING

Calamari, or baby squid, cook very quickly; be sure to turn and baste them often and take care not to overcook them.

INGREDIENTS

1¼ pounds baby squid, cleaned
1 garlic clove, crushed
3 plum tomatoes, skinned and chopped
8 sun-dried tomatoes in oil, drained and chopped
4 tablespoons chopped fresh basil, plus extra, to serve
4 tablespoons fresh white bread crumbs
3 tablespoons olive oil
1 tablespoon red wine vinegar
salt and freshly ground black pepper
lemon juice, to serve

SERVES 4

1 Remove the tentacles from the squid and roughly chop them; leave the main part of the squid whole.

2 Mix together the crushed garlic, plum tomatoes, sun-dried tomatoes, chopped fresh basil and bread crumbs. Stir in 1 tablespoon of the olive oil and the vinegar. Season with plenty of salt and freshly ground black pepper. Soak some wooden toothpicks in water for 10 minutes before use, to prevent them from burning on the grill.

3 Using a teaspoon, fill the squid with the stuffing mixture. Secure the open ends with the toothpicks to hold the stuffing mixture in place.

4 Brush the squid with the remaining olive oil and cook over a medium-hot grill for 4–5 minutes, turning often. Sprinkle with lemon juice and extra chopped fresh basil to serve.

Sardines with Warm Herb Salsa

Plain grilling is the very best way to cook fresh sardines. Served with this luscious herb salsa, the only other essential item is fresh, crusty bread, to mop up the tasty juices.

INGREDIENTS

12–16 fresh sardines
oil, for brushing
juice of 1 lemon

For the salsa
1 tablespoon butter
4 scallions, chopped
1 garlic clove, finely chopped
rind of 1 lemon
2 tablespoons finely chopped fresh parsley
2 tablespoons finely snipped fresh chives
2 tablespoons finely chopped fresh basil
2 tablespoon green olive paste
2 teaspoons balsamic vinegar
salt and freshly ground black pepper

Serves 4

1 To clean the sardines, use a pair of small kitchen scissors to slit the fish along the belly and pull out the intestines. Wipe the fish with paper towels and then arrange on a grill rack.

2 To make the salsa, melt the butter in a small pan and gently sauté the scallions and garlic for about 2 minutes, shaking the pan occasionally, until softened but not browned.

3 Add the lemon rind and remaining salsa ingredients to the scallions and garlic in the pan and keep warm on the edge of the grill, stirring occasionally. Do not allow to boil.

4 Brush the sardines lightly with oil and sprinkle with lemon juice, salt and pepper. Cook for about 2 minutes on each side, over moderate heat. Serve with the warm salsa and crusty bread.

Charbroiled Tuna with Fiery Pepper Puree

Tuna is an oily fish that grills well and is meaty enough to combine successfully with strong flavors—even hot chili, as in this red pepper purée, which is excellent served with crusty bread.

Ingredients

4 tuna steaks, about 6 ounces each
finely grated rind and juice of 1 lime
2 tablespoons olive oil
salt and freshly ground black pepper
lime wedges and crusty bread, to serve

For the pepper purée
2 red bell peppers, halved
3 tablespoons olive oil, plus extra for brushing
1 small onion
2 garlic cloves, crushed
2 fresh red chilies
1 slice white bread without crusts, diced
salt

Serves 4

1 Trim any skin from the tuna and place the steaks in a single layer in a wide dish. Sprinkle with the lime rind and juice, olive oil, salt and black pepper. Cover with plastic wrap and chill in the refrigerator until needed.

Cook's Tip

The pepper purée can be made ahead: cook the peppers and onion under a hot broiler and refrigerate them until you cook the fish.

2 To make the pepper purée, brush the pepper halves with a little olive oil and cook them, skin side down, on a hot grill, until the skin is charred and blackened. Place the onion in its skin on the grill and cook until browned, turning it occasionally.

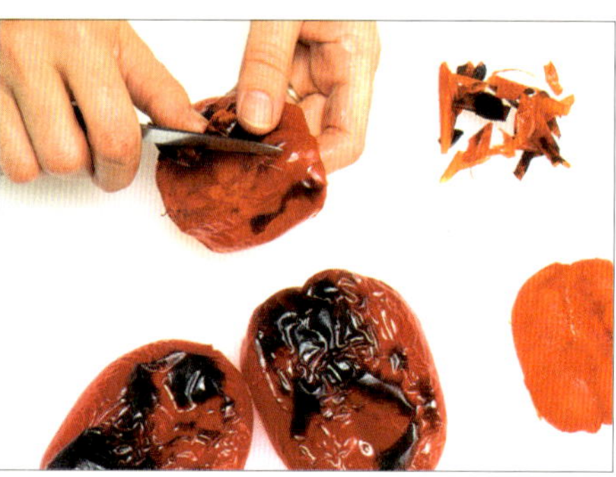

3 Set aside the peppers and onion until cool enough to handle, then remove the skins, using a sharp knife.

4 Place the cooked peppers and onion with the garlic, chilies, bread and olive oil in a food processor. Process until smooth. Add salt to taste.

5 Drain the tuna steaks from the marinade and cook them on a hot grill for 8–10 minutes, turning once, until golden brown. Serve the steaks with the pepper purée and lime wedges, and crusty bread if desired.

Mackerel Kebabs with Sweet Pepper Salad

Mackerel is an excellent fish for grilling because its natural oils keep it moist and tasty. This recipe combines mackerel with peppers and tomatoes in a flavorful summer salad.

Ingredients

4 medium mackerel, about 8 ounces each, filleted
2 small red onions, cut into wedges
2 tablespoons chopped fresh marjoram
4 tablespoons dry white wine
3 tablespoons olive oil
juice of 1 lime

For the Salad

1 red bell pepper
1 yellow bell pepper
1 small red onion
2 large plum tomatoes
1 tablespoon chopped fresh marjoram
2 teaspoons balsamic vinegar
salt and freshly ground black pepper

Serves 4

1 Thread each mackerel fillet onto a skewer, with an onion wedge on each end. Arrange the skewers in a dish.

2 Mix together the marjoram, wine, oil and lime juice and spoon over the fish. Cover and chill in the refrigerator for at least 30 minutes, turning once.

3 To make the salad, quarter and seed both peppers and halve the onion. Place the peppers and onion, skin side down, with the whole tomatoes on a hot grill and cook until the skins are blackened and charred.

4 Remove the vegetables from the grill and set aside until they are cool enough to handle. Use a sharp knife to peel off and discard the skins.

5 Chop the vegetables roughly and put them in a bowl. Stir in the marjoram and balsamic vinegar and season to taste. Toss thoroughly.

6 Remove the kebabs from the refrigerator and cook on a hot grill for 10–12 minutes, turning occasionally and basting with the marinade. Serve with the pepper salad.

Cook's Tip

Other oily fish can be used for this dish: try fillets or cubes of herring, rainbow trout or salmon, instead.

Grilled Scallops with Lime Butter

Fresh scallops cook quickly, so they're ideal for barbecues. This recipe combines them simply with lime and fennel.

INGREDIENTS

1 fennel bulb
2 limes
12 large scallops, cleaned
1 egg yolk
6 tablespoons melted butter
olive oil for brushing
salt and freshly ground black pepper

SERVES 4

1 Trim any feathery leaves from the fennel and reserve them. Slice the bulb lengthwise into thin wedges.

2 Cut one lime into wedges. Finely grate the rind and squeeze the juice from the other lime; toss half the juice and rind with the scallops. Season well with salt and fresh black pepper.

3 Place the egg yolk and remaining lime rind and juice in a small bowl and whisk until pale and smooth.

4 Gradually whisk in the melted butter and continue whisking until thick and smooth. Finely chop the reserved fennel leaves and stir them in, with seasoning to taste.

5 Brush the fennel wedges with olive oil and cook them on a hot grill for 3–4 minutes, turning once.

6 Add the scallops and cook for another 3–4 minutes, turning once. Serve with the lime and fennel butter and the lime wedges.

Cook's Tip

If the scallops are small, you may wish to thread them onto flat skewers to make turning them easier.

Trout with Bacon

The smoky, savory flavor of crisp grilled bacon perfectly complements the delicate flesh of the trout in this simple dish.

INGREDIENTS

4 trout, cleaned and gutted
1 tablespoon all-purpose flour
4 slices lean smoked bacon
2 tablespoons olive oil
juice of ½ lemon
salt and freshly ground black pepper

SERVES 4

1 Place the trout on a chopping board and pat dry with paper towels. Season the flour with the salt and freshly ground black pepper. Stretch the bacon slices out thinly using the back of a heavy kitchen knife.

2 Roll the fish in the seasoned flour mixture and wrap tightly in the bacon slices. Brush with olive oil and cook on a medium-hot grill for 10–15 minutes, turning once. Serve at once, with the lemon juice drizzled on top.

Mackerel with Tomatoes, Pesto and Onion

Rich, oily fish like mackerel needs a sharp, fresh-tasting sauce to go with it; this aromatic pesto is excellent drizzled over the top.

INGREDIENTS

4 mackerel, cleaned and gutted
2 tablespoons olive oil
4 ounces onion, roughly chopped
1 pound tomatoes, roughly chopped
salt and freshly ground black pepper

FOR THE PESTO

2 ounces pine nuts
2 tablespoons fresh basil leaves
2 garlic cloves, crushed
2 tablespoons freshly grated Parmesan cheese
2/3 cup extra virgin olive oil

SERVES 4

1 To make the pesto, place the pine nuts, fresh basil leaves and garlic in a food processor and blend to a rough paste. Add the Parmesan and, with the motor running, gradually add the oil.

2 Season the mackerel with plenty of salt and freshly ground black pepper and cook on a medium-hot grill for 12–15 minutes, turning once.

3 Meanwhile, heat the olive oil in a large, heavy saucepan and sauté the chopped onions until soft and golden brown.

4 Stir the chopped tomatoes into the contents of the saucepan and cook for 5 minutes. Serve the fish on top of the tomato mixture and top with a generous spoonful of the pesto.

SPICED FISH BAKED THAI STYLE

Banana leaves make a perfect, natural wrapping for grilled foods, but if they are not available you can use aluminum foil instead.

INGREDIENTS

4 red snapper or mullet, about 12 ounces each
banana leaves
1 lime
1 garlic clove, thinly sliced
2 scallions, thinly sliced
2 tablespoons Thai red curry paste
4 tablespoons coconut milk

SERVES 4

1 Clean the fish, removing the scales, and make several deep slashes in the side of each one with a sharp knife. Place each fish on a layer of banana leaves.

2 Thinly slice half the lime and tuck the slices into the slashes in the fish, with the slivers of garlic. Sprinkle the sliced scallions over the fish.

3 Grate the rind and squeeze the juice from the remaining lime half and mix with the curry paste and coconut milk. Spoon over the fish.

4 Wrap the leaves over the fish, enclosing them completely. Tie firmly with string and cook on a medium-hot grill for 15–20 minutes, turning occasionally. To serve, open up the parcels by cutting along the top edge with a knife and fanning out the leaves.

Red Mullet with Basil and Citrus

This Italian recipe is full of the warm, distinctive flavors of the Mediterranean. Serve the dish with plain boiled rice and a green salad, or with lots of fresh crusty bread.

INGREDIENTS

4 red mullet, about 8 ounces each, filleted
4 tablespoons olive oil
10 peppercorns, crushed
2 oranges, one peeled and sliced and one squeezed
1 lemon
1 tablespoon butter
2 drained canned anchovies, chopped
4 tablespoons shredded fresh basil
salt and freshly ground black pepper

SERVES 4

1 Place the fish fillets in a shallow dish in a single layer. Pour the olive oil over them and sprinkle with the crushed peppercorns. Lay the orange slices on top of the fish. Cover the dish with plastic wrap and marinate in the refrigerator for at least 4 hours.

2 Halve the lemon. Remove the skin and pith from one half using a small, sharp knife, and slice the flesh thinly. Squeeze the juice from the other half.

3 Drain the fish, reserving the marinade and orange slices, and cook on a medium-hot grill for 10–12 minutes, turning once and basting with the marinade.

4 Melt the butter in a saucepan with any remaining marinade. Add the chopped anchovies and cook until completely soft. Stir in the orange and lemon juice and allow to simmer on the edge of the grill until slightly reduced. Stir in the basil and check the seasoning. Pour the sauce over the fish and garnish with the reserved orange slices and the lemon slices.

Monkfish with Peppered Citrus Marinade

Monkfish is a firm, meaty fish that keeps its shape well when cooked on the grill. Serve with a green salad.

INGREDIENTS

2 monkfish tails, about 12 ounces each
1 lime
1 lemon
2 oranges
handful of fresh thyme sprigs
2 tablespoons olive oil
1 tablespoon mixed peppercorns, roughly crushed
salt and freshly ground black pepper

SERVES 4

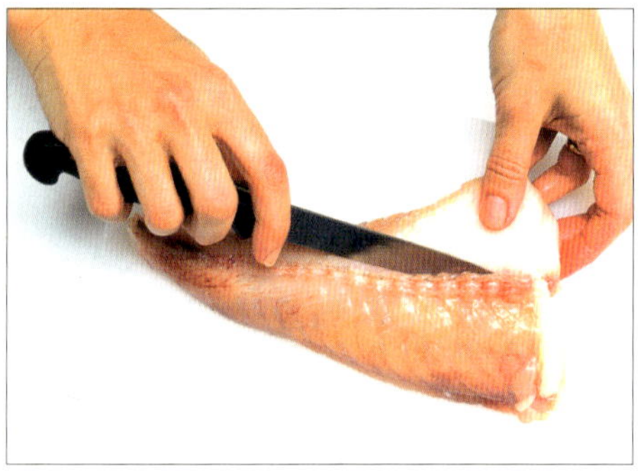

1 Using a sharp kitchen knife, remove any skin from the monkfish tails. Cut carefully down one side of the backbone, sliding the knife between the bone and the flesh, to remove the fillet on one side.

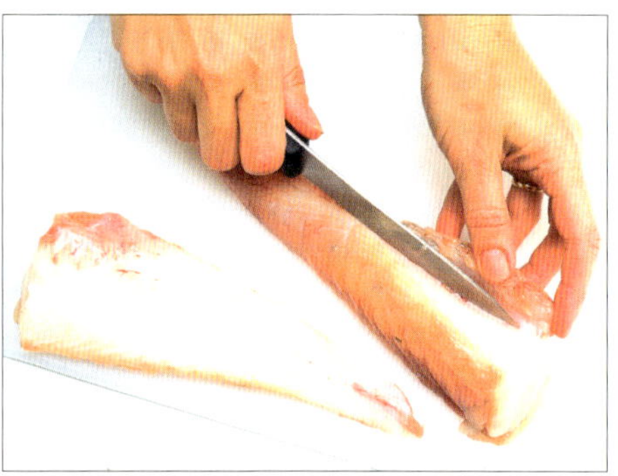

2 Turn the fish and repeat on the other side, to remove the second fillet. Repeat on the second tail. (If you prefer, you can ask your fishmonger to do this for you.) Lay the 4 fillets out flat on a chopping board.

3 Cut two slices from each of the citrus fruits and arrange them over 2 of the fillets. Add a few sprigs of fresh thyme and sprinkle with plenty of salt and freshly ground black pepper. Finely grate the rind from the remaining fruit and sprinkle it over the fish.

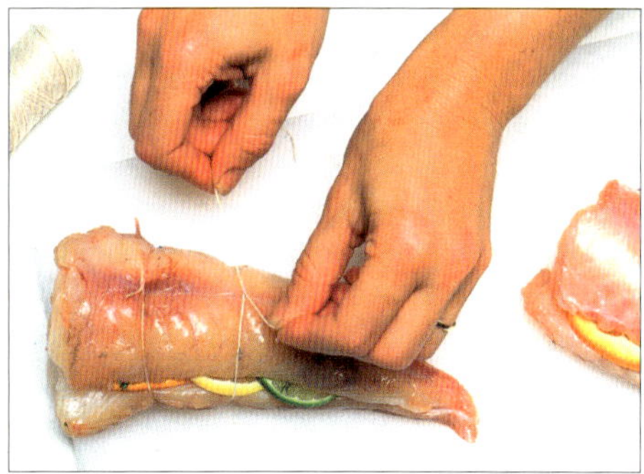

4 Lay the other 2 fillets on top and tie them firmly at intervals.

5 Squeeze the juice from the citrus fruits and mix it with the olive oil and more salt and pepper. Spoon over the fish. Cover with plastic wrap and marinate in the refrigerator for about 1 hour, turning occasionally and spooning the marinade over the fish.

6 Drain the monkfish, reserving the marinade, and sprinkle with the crushed peppercorns. Cook on a medium-hot grill for 15–20 minutes, basting with the marinade and turning occasionally, until the fish is evenly cooked. Serve immediately.

Fish Parcels

Sea bass is good for this recipe, but you could also use small whole trout or a white fish fillet such as cod or haddock.

INGREDIENTS

4 pieces sea bass fillet, or 4 small sea bass, about 1 pound each
olive oil for brushing
2 shallots, thinly sliced
1 garlic clove, chopped
1 tablespoon capers
6 sun-dried tomatoes, finely chopped
4 black olives, pitted and thinly sliced
grated rind and juice of 1 lemon
1 teaspoon paprika
salt and freshly ground black pepper

SERVES 4

1 Clean the fish if whole. Cut 4 squares of aluminum foil, large enough to enclose the fish; brush lightly with a little olive oil.

2 Place a piece of fish in the center of each piece of foil and season well with plenty of salt and pepper.

3 Sprinkle the shallots, chopped garlic, capers, tomatoes, sliced olives and lemon rind over the fish. Sprinkle with the lemon juice and paprika.

4 Fold over the foil to enclose the fish loosely, sealing the edges firmly so that none of the juices can escape during cooking. Place the parcels on a moderately hot grill and cook for 8–10 minutes. To serve, place each of the parcels on a plate and loosen the top to open.

Cook's Tip

These parcels can also be baked in the oven: Place them on a baking sheet and cook at 400°F for 15 to 20 minutes.

GRILLED SEA BASS WITH CITRUS FRUIT

Sea bass is a beautiful fish with a soft, dense texture and a delicate flavor. In this recipe it is complemented by citrus fruits and fruity olive oil.

INGREDIENTS

1 small grapefruit
1 orange
1 lemon
1 sea bass, 3–3½ pounds, cleaned and scaled
6 fresh basil sprigs
1 tablespoon olive oil, plus extra for brushing
4–6 shallots, halved
4 tablespoons dry white wine
1 tablespoon butter
salt and freshly ground black pepper
fresh dill, to garnish

SERVES 6

1 Using a vegetable peeler, remove the rind from the grapefruit, orange and lemon. Cut into thin julienne strips. Peel the pith from the fruits and, working over a bowl to catch the juices, cut out the segments from the grapefruit and the orange and set aside for the garnish. Slice the lemon thickly.

2 Season the cavity of the fish with salt and pepper and slash the flesh 3 times on each side. Reserving a few basil sprigs for the garnish, fill the cavity with the remaining basil, the lemon slices and half the julienne strips of citrus rind. Brush with olive oil and cook on a medium-low grill for about 20 minutes, basting occasionally and turning once.

3 Meanwhile, heat 1 tablespoon olive oil in a pan and cook the shallots gently until soft. Add the wine and 2–3 tablespoons of the fruit juice to the pan. Bring to a boil over high heat, stirring. Stir in the remaining julienne strips of rind and boil for 2–3 minutes, then whisk in the butter.

4 When the fish is cooked, transfer it to a serving dish. Remove and discard the stuffing. Spoon the shallots and sauce around the fish and garnish with fresh dill sprigs, the reserved basil and segments of grapefruit and orange.

Grilled Sea Bass with Fennel

The classic combination of sea bass and fennel works particularly well when the fish is cooked over charcoal. Traditionally, fennel twigs are used, but this version of the dish uses fennel seeds.

INGREDIENTS

1 sea bass, 3–3 ½ pounds, cleaned and scaled
4 tablespoons olive oil
2 teaspoons fennel seeds
2 large fennel bulbs
4 tablespoons Pernod
salt and freshly ground black pepper

SERVES 6

1 Make 4 deep slashes in each side of the fish. Brush the fish with olive oil and season well with salt and freshly ground black pepper. Sprinkle the fennel seeds in the cavity and slashes of the fish. Cook on a low grill for 20 minutes, basting occasionally and turning once.

2 Meanwhile, trim and slice the fennel bulbs thinly, reserving any leafy fronds to use as a garnish. Brush the slices with olive oil and grill for 8–10 minutes, turning the fish occasionally, until tender. Remove the fish from the heat and keep it warm.

3 Scatter the fennel slices on a serving plate. Lay the fish on top and garnish with the reserved fennel fronds.

4 When ready to eat, heat the Pernod in a small pan on the side of the grill, light it and pour it, flaming, over the fish. Serve at once.

Mexican Barbecued Salmon

The sauce for this dish is vibrant with hot, sweet and sour flavors that permeate the fish before and during cooking.

INGREDIENTS

1 small red onion
1 garlic clove
6 plum tomatoes
2 tablespoons butter
3 tablespoons ketchup
2 tablespoons Dijon mustard
2 tablespoons dark brown sugar
1 tablespoon honey
1 tablespoon cayenne pepper
1 tablespoon ancho chili powder
1 tablespoon paprika
1 tablespoon Worcestershire sauce
4 salmon fillets, about 6 ounces each

SERVES 4

1 Using a sharp knife, finely chop the red onion and finely dice the garlic.

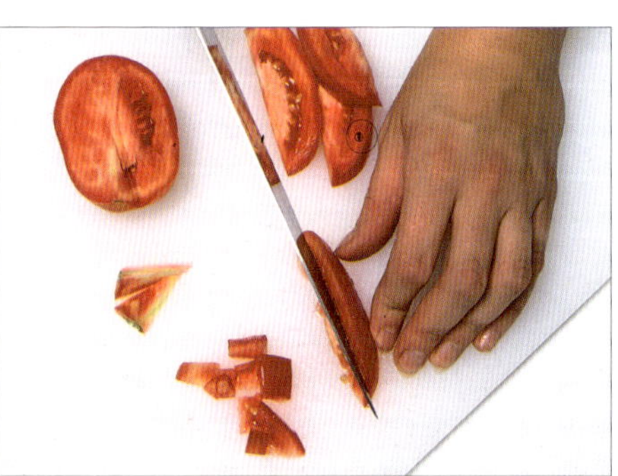

2 Next, dice the plum tomatoes finely and set them aside.

3 Melt the butter in a large, heavy saucepan and gently cook the onion and garlic until translucent.

4 Add the tomatoes to the saucepan and allow to simmer for 15 minutes.

5 Add the remaining ingredients, excluding the salmon, and simmer for another 20 minutes. Pour the mixture into a food processor and blend until smooth. Set aside to cool.

6 Brush the salmon with the sauce, and chill for at least 2 hours. Cook on a hot grill for 6 minutes, basting with the sauce and turning once.

Vegetarian Dishes and Vegetables

Vegetables cooked on the grill acquire a richness and depth of flavor that will add an extra dimension to your meal. There are lots of ideas here for vegetable accompaniments to meat and fish dishes, as well as for substantial main dishes that everyone, vegetarian or not, will love. All vegetables can be cooked in aluminum foil parcels, but many are ideally suited to cooking on the grill: jacket potatoes, bell peppers, eggplant and corn on the cob are irresistible cooked over charcoal, or you can spear a mixture of vegetables onto skewers to make colorful and delicious kebabs. Charbroiled vegetables can also be cooled and made into fabulous salads. They certainly shouldn't be an afterthought on your barbecue menu.

SWEET AND SOUR VEGETABLES WITH PANEER

The Indian cheese used in this recipe, called paneer, can be bought at Asian stores, or you can use tofu in its place. Paneer has a good firm texture and cooks very well on the grill.

INGREDIENTS

1 green and 1 yellow bell pepper, cut into squares
8 cherry, or 4 medium, tomatoes
8 cauliflower florets
8 fresh or canned pineapple chunks
8 cubes paneer

FOR THE SEASONED OIL

1 tablespoon soybean oil
2 tablespoons lemon juice
1 teaspoon salt
1 teaspoon freshly ground black pepper
1 tablespoon honey
2 tablespoons chili sauce

SERVES 4

1 Thread the prepared vegetables, pineapple and paneer cubes onto 4 skewers, alternating the ingredients.

2 Mix together all the ingredients for the seasoned oil. If the mixture seems a little too thick, add 1 tablespoon water. Brush the vegetables with the seasoned oil.

3 Cook on a hot grill or under the broiler for 10 minutes, turning the skewers often and basting with the seasoned oil. Sprinkle with pepper and serve on a bed of plain boiled rice.

VEGETABLE KEBABS WITH PEPPERCORN SAUCE

Vegetables invariably taste good when cooked on the grill. You can include other vegetables in these kebabs, depending on what is available at the time.

INGREDIENTS

24 mushrooms
16 cherry tomatoes
16 large fresh basil leaves
2 zucchini, cut into 16 thick slices
16 large fresh mint leaves
1 large red bell pepper, cut into 16 squares

TO BASTE

8 tablespoons (1 stick) melted butter
1 garlic clove, crushed
1 tablespoon crushed green peppercorns
salt

FOR THE GREEN PEPPERCORN SAUCE

4 tablespoons butter
3 tablespoons brandy
1 cup heavy cream
1 teaspoon crushed green peppercorns

SERVES 4

1 Thread the vegetables and herbs onto 8 bamboo skewers that have been soaked in water to prevent them from burning: Place the fresh basil leaves next to the tomatoes, and wrap the mint leaves around the zucchini slices.

2 Mix the basting ingredients in a bowl and baste the kebabs thoroughly. Cook the skewers on a medium-hot grill, turning and basting regularly, until the vegetables are just cooked—this should take 5–7 minutes.

3 Heat the butter for the green peppercorn sauce in a frying pan, then add the brandy and light it. When the flames have died down, stir in the cream and the peppercorns. Cook for 2 minutes, stirring constantly. Serve the sauce with the grilled kebabs.

POTATO AND CHEESE POLPETTE

These little morsels of potato and Greek feta cheese, flavored with dill and lemon juice, are excellent when grilled, or they can be tossed in flour and fried in olive oil.

INGREDIENTS

1¼ pounds potatoes
4 ounces feta cheese
4 scallions, chopped
3 tablespoons chopped fresh dill
1 egg, beaten
1 tablespoon lemon juice
2 tablespoons olive oil
salt and freshly ground black pepper

SERVES 4

1 Boil the potatoes in their skins in salted water until soft. Drain, then peel while still warm. Place in a bowl and mash. Crumble the feta cheese into the potatoes and add the scallions, dill, egg and lemon juice and season with pepper and a little salt. Stir well.

2 Cover the mixture and chill until firm. Divide the mixture into walnut-size balls, then flatten them slightly. Brush lightly with olive oil. Arrange the polpette on a grill rack and cook on a medium grill, turning once, until golden brown. Serve at once.

GRILLED GOAT CHEESE PIZZA

Pizzas cooked on the grill have a beautifully crisp and golden crust. The combination of goat cheese and red onion in this recipe makes for a flavorful main course dish.

2 Brush the dough round with olive oil and place, oiled side down, on a medium grill. Cook for 6–8 minutes, until firm and golden underneath. Brush the uncooked side with olive oil and turn the pizza over.

3 Mix together the tomato sauce and pesto and quickly spread over the cooked side of the pizza, to within about ½ inch of the edge. Arrange the onion, tomatoes and cheese on top and sprinkle with salt and pepper.

INGREDIENTS

5-ounce package pizza-dough mix
olive oil, for brushing
⅔ cup tomato sauce
2 tablespoons tomato pesto
1 small red onion, thinly sliced
8 cherry tomatoes, halved
4 ounces firm goat cheese, thinly sliced
handful shredded fresh basil leaves
salt and freshly ground black pepper

SERVES 4

1 Make up the pizza dough according to the directions on the package. Roll out the dough on a lightly floured surface to a round about 10 inches in diameter.

4 Cook the pizza for 10 minutes more, until golden brown and crisp. Sprinkle with fresh basil and serve.

Grilled Eggplant Parcels

These little bundles of tomatoes, mozzarella cheese and basil, wrapped in slices of eggplant, taste delicious cooked on the grill.

INGREDIENTS

2 large, long eggplants
8 ounces mozzarella cheese
2 plum tomatoes
16 large fresh basil leaves
2 tablespoons olive oil
salt and freshly ground black pepper

FOR THE DRESSING

4 tablespoons olive oil
1 teaspoon balsamic vinegar
1 tablespoon sun-dried tomato paste
1 tablespoon lemon juice

FOR THE GARNISH

2 tablespoons toasted pine nuts
torn fresh basil leaves

SERVES 4

1 Remove the stalks from the eggplants and cut them lengthwise into thin slices using a mandoline or long-bladed knife—aim to get 16 slices total, each about 1/4 inch thick, not counting the first and last slices.

2 Bring a large saucepan of salted water to the boil and cook the eggplant slices for about 2 minutes, until just softened. Drain the slices, then pat them dry on paper towels.

3 Cut the mozzarella cheese into 8 slices. Cut each tomato into 8 slices, not counting the first and last slices. Take 2 eggplant slices and arrange in a cross. Place a slice of tomato in the center, season, then add a basil leaf, followed by a slice of mozzarella, another basil leaf, another slice of tomato and more seasoning.

4 Fold the ends of the eggplant slices around the filling to make a neat parcel. Repeat with the rest of the assembled ingredients to make 8 parcels. Chill the parcels in the refrigerator for about 20 minutes.

5 To make the tomato dressing, whisk together the olive oil, vinegar, sun-dried tomato paste and lemon juice. Season to taste with plenty of salt and freshly ground black pepper.

6 Brush the parcels with olive oil and cook on a hot grill for about 10 minutes, turning once, until golden. Serve hot, with the dressing, sprinkled with pine nuts and fresh basil.

Vegetable Parcels with Flowery Butter

Nasturtium leaves and flowers are edible and have a distinctive peppery flavor. They make a pretty addition to a summer barbecue.

INGREDIENTS

7 ounces baby carrots
9 ounces yellow pattypan squash or summer squash
4 ounces baby corn
1 onion, thinly sliced
4 tablespoons butter, plus extra for greasing
finely grated rind of ½ lemon
6 young nasturtium leaves
4–8 nasturtium flowers
salt and freshly ground black pepper

SERVES 4

1 Trim the vegetables with a sharp knife, leaving them whole unless they are very large—if necessary, cut them into even-size pieces.

2 Divide the vegetables among 4 double-thickness squares of buttered aluminum foil and season well.

3 Mix the butter with the lemon rind in a small bowl. Roughly chop the nasturtium leaves and add them to the butter. Place a generous spoonful of the butter on each pile of vegetables in the squares of foil.

4 Fold over the foil and seal the edges to make a neat parcel. Cook on a medium-hot grill for 30 minutes, until the vegetables are tender. Open the parcels and top each with one or two nasturtium flowers. Serve at once.

Spinach with Raisins and Pine Nuts

Raisins and pine nuts are frequent partners in Spanish dishes. In this recipe, they are tossed with wilted spinach and croutons; the mixture can be cooked quickly in a flameproof pan on the grill.

INGREDIENTS

1/3 cup raisins
1 thick slice crusty white bread
3 tablespoons olive oil
1/3 cup pine nuts
1 1/4 pounds young spinach, stalks removed
2 garlic cloves, crushed
salt and freshly ground black pepper

Serves 4

1 Put the raisins in a bowl, cover with boiling water and let soak for 10 minutes. Drain and set aside.

2 Cut the bread into cubes and discard the crusts. Heat 2 tablespoons of the olive oil in a large frying pan and fry the bread until golden brown.

3 Heat the remaining oil and fry the pine nuts, on the grill or stove, until beginning to color. Add the spinach and garlic and cook quickly, turning the spinach until it has just wilted. Toss in the raisins and season lightly with salt and pepper. Transfer to a serving dish. Scatter with croutons and serve.

BAKED STUFFED ZUCCHINI

The tangy goat cheese stuffing contrasts well with the very delicate flavor of the zucchini in this recipe. Wrap the zucchini in aluminum foil and bake them in the embers of the fire.

INGREDIENTS

8 small zucchini, about 1 pound total weight
1 tablespoon olive oil, plus extra for brushing
3–4 ounces goat cheese, cut into thin strips
a few sprigs of fresh mint, finely chopped, plus extra to garnish
freshly ground black pepper

SERVES 4

1 Cut 8 pieces of aluminum foil large enough to encase each zucchini and lightly brush with olive oil. Trim the zucchini and cut a thin slit along the length of each.

2 Insert pieces of goat cheese into the slits. Add a little chopped mint and sprinkle with the oil and black pepper.

3 Wrap each zucchini in foil, place in the embers of the fire and bake for about 25 minutes, until tender.

Cook's Tip

While almost any cheese can be used in this recipe, mild cheeses, such as Cheddar or mozzarella, will best allow the flavor of the zucchini to be appreciated.

CORN ON THE COB IN A GARLIC BUTTER CRUST

Whether you are catering for vegetarians or serving this with meat dishes, it will disappear in a flash. The charred garlic butter crust adds a new dimension to the corn.

INGREDIENTS

6 ears of fresh corn
½ pound (2 sticks) butter
2 tablespoons olive oil
2 garlic cloves, crushed
1 cup whole-wheat bread crumbs
1 tablespoon chopped fresh parsley
salt and freshly ground black pepper

SERVES 6

1 Pull off the husks and silks and cook the corn in a large saucepan of boiling salted water until tender. Drain and set aside to cool.

2 Melt the butter in a saucepan, add the olive oil, crushed garlic, salt and freshly ground black pepper, and stir to blend. Pour the mixture into a shallow dish. In another shallow dish blend the bread crumbs and chopped fresh parsley. Roll the corn in the melted butter mixture and then in the bread crumbs until they are well coated.

3 Cook the corn on a hot grill for about 10 minutes, turning frequently, until the bread crumbs are golden brown.

BAKED SQUASH WITH PARMESAN

Almost all types of squash are suitable for grilling, and they are extremely easy to deal with: Simply wrap them in aluminum foil and place them in the hot embers until they soften.

INGREDIENTS

2 acorn or butternut squash, about 1 pound each
1 tablespoon olive oil
4 tablespoons butter, melted
1 cup grated Parmesan cheese
4 tablespoons pine nuts, toasted
salt and freshly ground black pepper
1/2 teaspoon freshly grated nutmeg

SERVES 4

1 Cut the squash in half and scoop out the seeds with a spoon.

2 Brush the cut surfaces with oil and sprinkle with salt and black pepper.

3 Wrap each squash in foil and place in the embers of the fire. Cook for 25–30 minutes, until tender. Turn the parcels occasionally so that the squash cook evenly.

4 When they are cool enough to handle, unwrap the squash from the foil parcels and scoop out the flesh, leaving the skins intact.

5 Dice the flesh, then stir in the melted butter. Add the Parmesan, pine nuts, salt and pepper. Toss well to mix.

6 Spoon the mixture back into the shells. Sprinkle with nutmeg to serve.

Cook's Tip

Spaghetti squash can also be cooked in this way. Just scoop out the spaghetti-like strands and toss with butter and Parmesan cheese.

Summer Vegetables with Yogurt Pesto

Grilled vegetables make a meal on their own, or are delicious served as a Mediterranean-style accompaniment to grilled meats and fish.

INGREDIENTS

2 small eggplants
2 large zucchini
1 red bell pepper
1 yellow bell pepper
1 fennel bulb
1 red onion
olive oil, for brushing
salt and freshly ground black pepper

FOR THE YOGURT PESTO
2/3 cup strained plain yogurt
3 tablespoons pesto

SERVES 4

1 Cut the eggplants into 1/2-inch slices. Sprinkle with salt and let drain for about 30 minutes. Rinse well in cold running water and pat dry.

2 Use a sharp kitchen knife to cut the zucchini in half lengthwise. Cut the peppers in half, removing the seeds but leaving the stalks in place.

3 Slice the fennel bulb and the red onion into thick wedges, using a sharp kitchen knife.

4 Stir the yogurt and pesto lightly together in a bowl, to make a marbled sauce. Spoon the yogurt pesto into a serving bowl and set aside.

5 Arrange the vegetables on the hot grill, brush generously with olive oil and sprinkle with plenty of salt and freshly ground black pepper.

6 Cook the vegetables until golden brown and tender, turning occasionally. The eggplants and peppers will take 6–8 minutes to cook, the zucchini, onion and fennel 4–5 minutes. Serve the vegetables as soon as they are cooked, with the yogurt pesto.

Cook's Tip

Baby vegetables make excellent candidates for grilling whole; look for baby eggplants and peppers, in particular. There's no need to salt the eggplants if they're small.

POTATO SKEWERS WITH MUSTARD DIP

Potatoes cooked on the grill have a good flavor and crisp skin. These skewers are served with a thick, garlic-rich dip.

INGREDIENTS

2¼ pounds small new potatoes
7 ounces shallots, halved
2 tablespoons olive oil
1 tablespoon sea salt

FOR THE MUSTARD DIP

4 garlic cloves, crushed
2 egg yolks
2 tablespoons lemon juice
1¼ cups extra virgin olive oil
2 teaspoons whole-grain mustard
salt and freshly ground black pepper

SERVES 4

1 To make the mustard dip, place the garlic, egg yolks and lemon juice in a blender or food processor and process for a few seconds, until smooth.

2 With the motor running, add the oil until the mixture forms a thick cream. Add the mustard and season.

3 Parboil the potatoes in salted boiling water for about 5 minutes. Drain well and then thread them onto metal skewers with the shallots.

4 Brush with olive oil and sprinkle with sea salt. Cook for 10–12 minutes over a hot grill, turning often, until tender. Serve with the mustard dip.

Potato Wedges with Garlic and Rosemary

Toss the potato wedges in fragrant, garlicky olive oil with chopped fresh rosemary, before grilling them over the coals.

INGREDIENTS

1½ pounds medium potatoes
1 tablespoon olive oil
2 garlic cloves, thinly sliced
4 tablespoons chopped fresh rosemary
salt and freshly ground black pepper

Serves 4

1 Cut each potato into 4 wedges and parboil in boiling salted water for 5 minutes. Drain well.

2 Toss the potatoes in the olive oil with the garlic, rosemary and black pepper. Arrange on a grill rack.

3 Cook the potatoes on a hot grill for about 15 minutes, turning occasionally, until crisp and golden brown.

Salads and Accompaniments

Cool salads are a perfect foil to grilled food, but they should have assertive characters of their own. The recipes that follow include some marvelous sunny, Mediterranean flavors that taste especially good on summer days, and a selection of them would be perfect as part of a buffet for a party. Don't forget that you can use the grill to broil ingredients such as tomatoes, bell peppers, eggplant and radicchio – it will give them an intense, smoky flavor that will pervade the whole salad.

Curly Endive Salad with Bacon

When they are in season, young dandelion leaves could be included in this hearty French salad. If you wish, sprinkle the salad with chopped hard-boiled egg.

INGREDIENTS

6 cups curly endive or escarole leaves
5–6 tablespoons extra virgin olive oil
6-ounce piece of smoked bacon, diced
thick slice of white bread, cubed
1 small garlic clove, finely chopped
1 tablespoon red wine vinegar
2 teaspoons Dijon mustard
salt and freshly ground black pepper

SERVES 4

1 Tear the lettuce leaves into bite-size pieces and put them in a large salad bowl. Set the bowl aside.

2 Heat 1 tablespoon oil in a pan over medium heat and add the bacon. Fry until browned. Remove the bacon and drain on paper towels.

3 Add another 2 tablespoons oil to the pan and fry the bread cubes over medium heat, turning frequently, until browned. Remove the bread cubes with a slotted spoon and drain on paper towels. Discard any remaining fat.

4 Stir the garlic, vinegar and mustard into the pan with the remaining oil and warm through. Season to taste. Pour the dressing over the salad and sprinkle with the fried bacon and croutons.

PEPPERS WITH TOMATOES AND ANCHOVIES

This is a Sicilian-style salad full of warm Mediterranean flavors. The salad improves if it is made and dressed an hour or two before serving.

INGREDIENTS

1 red bell pepper
1 yellow bell pepper
4 ripe plum tomatoes, sliced
2 canned anchovies, drained and chopped
4 sun-dried tomatoes in oil, drained and sliced
1 tablespoon capers, drained
1 tablespoon pine nuts
1 garlic clove, very finely sliced

FOR THE DRESSING

5 tablespoons extra virgin olive oil
1 tablespoon balsamic vinegar
1 teaspoon lemon juice
chopped fresh mixed herbs
salt and freshly ground black pepper

SERVES 4

1 Cut the peppers in half and remove the seeds and stalks. Cut into quarters and cook, skin side down, over a hot grill or under the broiler until the skin chars. Transfer to a bowl and let cool. Peel the peppers and cut into strips.

2 Arrange the peppers and fresh tomatoes on a serving dish. Sprinkle the anchovies, sun-dried tomatoes, capers, pine nuts and garlic on top.

3 To make the dressing, mix together the olive oil, vinegar, lemon juice and chopped fresh herbs and season with plenty of salt and pepper. Pour the dressing over the salad before serving.

SWEET AND SOUR ONION SALAD

This recipe for tangy glazed onions in the Provençal style makes an unusual and flavorful accompaniment to grilled steaks.

INGREDIENTS

1 pound baby onions, peeled
1/4 cup wine vinegar
3 tablespoons olive oil
3 tablespoons sugar
3 tablespoons tomato paste
1 bay leaf
2 parsley sprigs
1/2 cup raisins
salt and freshly ground black pepper

SERVES 6

1 Put all the ingredients in a pan with 1 1/4 cups water. Bring to a boil and simmer gently, uncovered, for 45 minutes, or until the onions are tender and the liquid has evaporated.

2 Remove the bay leaf and parsley from the pan and check the seasoning. Transfer the contents of the pan to a large serving dish. Serve the salad at room temperature.

SPICED EGGPLANT SALAD

Serve this Middle Eastern–influenced salad with warm pita bread as an appetizer, or as an accompaniment to any number of grilled main-course dishes.

INGREDIENTS

2 small eggplants, sliced
5 tablespoons olive oil
1/4 cup red wine vinegar
2 garlic cloves, crushed
1 tablespoon lemon juice
1/2 teaspoon ground cumin
1/2 teaspoon ground coriander
1/2 cucumber, thinly sliced
2 ripe, flavorful tomatoes, thinly sliced
2 tablespoons plain yogurt
salt and freshly ground black pepper
chopped flat-leaf parsley, to garnish

SERVES 4

1 Brush the eggplant slices lightly with some of the olive oil and cook over a hot grill or under the broiler until golden and tender, turning once. Allow the slices to cool slightly, then cut them into quarters.

2 Mix the remaining olive oil with the vinegar, crushed garlic, lemon juice, and ground cumin and coriander. Season with plenty of salt and pepper and mix thoroughly. Add the warm eggplant, stir well and chill for at least 2 hours. Add the cucumber and tomatoes. Transfer the salad to a serving dish and spoon the yogurt on top. Garnish with chopped parsley to serve.

WARM FAVA BEAN AND FETA SALAD

This recipe is loosely based on a typical medley of fresh-tasting salad ingredients—fava beans, tomatoes and feta cheese. It's lovely either warm or cold.

INGREDIENTS

2 pounds fresh fava beans, or 12 ounces frozen fava beans
4 tablespoons olive oil
6 ounces plum tomatoes, halved, or quartered if large
4 garlic cloves, crushed
4 ounces firm feta cheese, cut into chunks
3 tablespoons chopped fresh dill, plus extra to garnish
12 black olives
salt and freshly ground black pepper

SERVES 4–6

1 Shell the fava beans, then cook them in boiling, salted water until they are just tender. Drain and set aside.

2 Meanwhile, heat the olive oil in a heavy frying pan and add the tomatoes and garlic. Cook until the tomatoes are beginning to color.

3 Add the feta to the frying pan and toss the ingredients together for 1 minute. Mix with the drained beans, dill, olives and salt and pepper. Serve garnished with the chopped fresh dill.

FAVA BEAN, MUSHROOM AND CHORIZO SALAD

This salad can be served as a first course or as part of a buffet menu. Prepare it a day in advance and store it in the refrigerator until needed.

INGREDIENTS

8 ounces shelled fava beans
6 ounces chorizo sausage
4 tablespoons extra virgin olive oil
8 ounces crimini mushrooms, sliced
handful of fresh chives
salt and freshly ground black pepper

SERVES 4

1 Cook the beans in a large saucepan of boiling, salted water until just tender. Drain and refresh under cold running water. If the beans are large, peel away the tough outer skins.

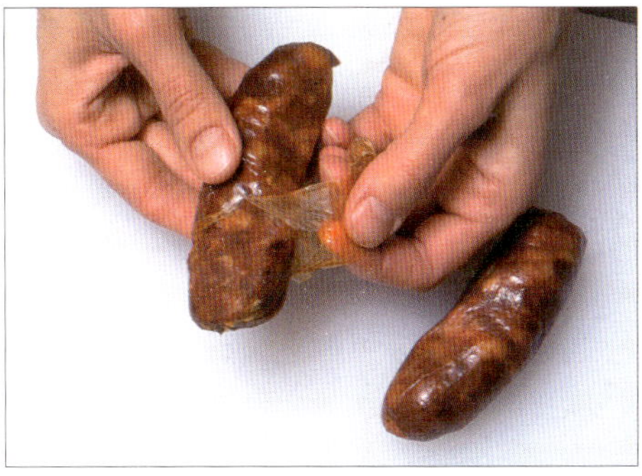

2 Remove the skin from the chorizo and cut it into small chunks. Heat the oil in a frying pan, add the chorizo and cook for 2 minutes. Empty into a bowl with the mushrooms, mix well and set aside to cool.

3 Chop half the chives and stir the beans and chopped chives into the mushroom mixture. Season to taste. Serve the salad at room temperature, garnished with the remaining chives.

Baby Eggplants with Raisins and Pine Nuts

This is a recipe with an Italian influence, in a style that would have been familiar in Renaissance times. If possible, make it a day in advance, to allow the sweet and sour flavors to develop.

INGREDIENTS

12 baby eggplants, halved
1 cup extra virgin olive oil
juice of 1 lemon
2 tablespoons balsamic vinegar
3 cloves
1/3 cup pine nuts
2 tablespoons raisins
1 tablespoon sugar
1 bay leaf
large pinch of crushed red pepper
salt and freshly ground black pepper

Serves 4

1 Brush the eggplants with olive oil and cook over a hot grill for about 10 minutes, until charred, turning once.

2 To make the dressing, combine the remaining olive oil with the lemon juice, vinegar, cloves, pine nuts, raisins, sugar and bay leaf. Add the red pepper, salt and pepper and mix well.

3 Place the hot eggplants in an earthenware or glass bowl and pour the dressing over them. Let cool, turning the eggplants once or twice. Serve the salad at room temperature.

Radicchio, Artichoke and Walnut Salad

The distinctive, earthy taste of Jerusalem artichokes makes a lovely contrast to the sharp freshness of radicchio and lemon. Serve warm or cold as an accompaniment to grilled meats.

INGREDIENTS

1¼ pounds Jerusalem artichokes
grated rind and juice of 1 lemon
1 large head of radicchio or 5 ounces radicchio leaves
6 tablespoons walnut pieces
3 tablespoons walnut oil
coarse sea salt and freshly ground black pepper
flat-leaf parsley, to garnish

SERVES 4

1 Peel the artichokes and cut up any large ones so the pieces are the same size. Add to a pan of boiling salted water with half the lemon juice and cook for 5 minutes, until tender. Drain.

2 If using a whole radicchio, cut it into 8–10 wedges. Grill the wedges or leaves, with the pieces of artichoke, over a hot grill until the radicchio and artichokes begin to brown. Transfer to a warmed serving dish, sprinkle with the walnuts, and then pour the walnut oil over the salad.

3 Toss the salad with the remaining lemon juice and the lemon rind. Season with coarse sea salt and freshly ground black pepper and serve at once, garnished with fresh flat-leaf parsley.

Salsas, Dips and Marinades

The powerful flavors of grilled meat and fish call for spicy, lively accompaniments. Chunky salsas are ideal, with their intriguing combination of cool, crisp ingredients and fiery flavors. Tangy barbecue sauce is a more traditional alternative that children adore. For a subtler effect, melt a pat of butter flavored with herbs, garlic or anchovies over a plainly grilled steak or fish. This chapter also includes some appetizing dips to go with potato chips, bread sticks and crudités, and a selection of delicious marinades suitable for a wide variety of meat and fish.

Chunky Cherry Tomato Salsa

Succulent cherry tomatoes and refreshing cucumber form the base of this delicious dill-seasoned salsa. Prepare up to a day in advance and store in the refrigerator until needed.

INGREDIENTS

1 cucumber
1 teaspoon sea salt
1¼ pound cherry tomatoes
grated rind and juice of 1 lemon
3 tablespoons chili oil
½ teaspoon crushed red pepper
2 tablespoons chopped fresh dill
1 garlic clove, finely chopped
salt and freshly ground black pepper

SERVES 4

1 Trim the ends off the cucumber and cut it into 1-inch lengths, then cut each piece lengthwise into thin slices. Place in a colander and sprinkle with sea salt. Let sit for 5 minutes.

2 Rinse the cucumber slices under cold water and dry with paper towels.

3 Quarter the cherry tomatoes and place in a bowl with the cucumber.

4 Whisk together the lemon rind and juice, chili oil, crushed red pepper, dill and garlic. Season, then pour over the tomato and cucumber and toss well. Marinate for 2 hours before serving.

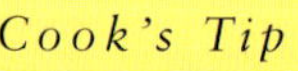

Cook's Tip

Try flavoring the salsa with other herbs: tarragon, cilantro or mint.

FIERY CITRUS SALSA

This unusual salsa makes a fantastic marinade for shellfish; it's also delicious drizzled over grilled meat.

INGREDIENTS

1 orange
1 green apple
2 fresh red chilies
1 garlic clove
8 fresh mint leaves
juice of 1 lemon
salt and freshly ground black pepper

SERVES 4

1 Using a sharp knife, remove the peel and pith from the orange and, working over a bowl to catch the juices, cut out the segments. Squeeze any remaining juice into the bowl.

2 Use a sharp kitchen knife to peel the apple and slice it into wedges. Remove and discard the apple core.

3 Halve the chilies and remove the seeds, then place them in a blender or food processor with the orange segments and juice, apple wedges, garlic and mint.

4 Process until smooth. With the motor running, slowly pour in the lemon juice. Season to taste with salt and freshly ground black pepper and serve immediately.

FRESH CORN SALSA

Serve this succulent salsa with grilled ham or pork, or with smoked meats. The charbroiled fresh corn makes the salsa particularly flavorful.

INGREDIENTS

2 ears of fresh corn
2 tablespoons melted butter
4 tomatoes
6 scallions, finely chopped
1 garlic clove, finely chopped
2 tablespoons lemon juice
2 tablespoons olive oil
red Tabasco sauce, to taste
salt and freshly ground black pepper

SERVES 4

1 Remove the husks and silks from the corn. Brush with the melted butter and gently grill or broil for about 20 minutes, turning occasionally, until tender and charred.

2 To remove the kernels, stand each ear upright on a chopping board and use a large, heavy knife to slice down its length. Put the kernels in a mixing bowl.

3 Skewer the tomatoes and hold them over the grill or broil them for about 2 minutes, turning, until the skin splits and wrinkles. Slip off the skins and dice the flesh. Add to the corn with the scallions and chopped garlic.

4 Stir the lemon juice and olive oil together, adding Tabasco, salt and black pepper to taste. Pour mixture over the salsa, stir well, cover and set aside to marinate at room temperature for 1–2 hours before serving.

Barbecue Sauce

Brush this sauce liberally over chicken pieces, chops or kebabs before cooking on the grill, or serve as a hot or cold accompaniment to hot dogs and hamburgers.

INGREDIENTS

2 tablespoons vegetable oil
1 large onion, chopped
2 garlic cloves, crushed
14-ounce can tomatoes
2 tablespoons Worcestershire sauce
1 tablespoon white wine vinegar
3 tablespoons honey
1 teaspoon mustard powder
½ teaspoon chili seasoning or mild chili powder
salt and freshly ground black pepper

Serves 4

1 Heat the vegetable oil in a large saucepan and fry the onions and garlic until soft and golden.

2 Stir in the remaining ingredients and simmer, uncovered, for 15–20 minutes, stirring occasionally. Remove the saucepan from the heat and allow to cool slightly.

3 Pour into a food processor or blender and process until smooth.

4 Press through a sieve if you like. Adjust the seasoning to taste.

CARAMELIZED ONION RELISH

Slow, gentle cooking reduces the onions to a soft, sweet relish, which would make a tasty addition to many barbecue menus.

2 Heat the butter and oil together in a large saucepan. Add the onions and sugar and cook very gently for 30 minutes over low heat, stirring occasionally, until reduced to a soft rich brown caramelized mixture.

3 Roughly chop the capers and stir them into the caramelized onions. Allow to cool completely.

INGREDIENTS

3 large onions
4 tablespoons butter
2 tablespoons olive oil
2 tablespoons light brown sugar
2 tablespoons capers
2 tablespoons chopped fresh parsley
salt and freshly ground black pepper

SERVES 4

1 Peel the onions and halve them vertically through the core, using a sharp knife. Slice them thinly.

4 Stir in the chopped fresh parsley and add salt and pepper to taste. Cover with plastic wrap and chill in the refrigerator until ready to serve.

PARSLEY BUTTER

This butter, or one of the variations below, makes a subtle accompaniment to grilled food, particularly fish with a delicate flavor.

INGREDIENTS

8 tablespoons softened butter
2 tablespoons finely chopped parsley
½ teaspoon lemon juice
cayenne pepper
salt and freshly ground black pepper

SERVES 4

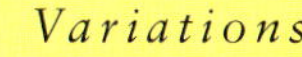

1 Beat the butter until creamy, then beat in the parsley, lemon juice and cayenne pepper, and season lightly.

2 Spread the butter 1/4 inch thick onto a piece of foil, chill, then cut into shapes with a knife or cookie cutter.

3 Alternatively, form the butter into a roll, wrap in plastic wrap or foil and chill. Cut off slices as required.

Variations

LEMON OR LIME BUTTER
Add 1 tablespoon finely grated lemon or lime rind and 1 tablespoon juice to the butter.

HERB BUTTER
Replace the parsley with 2 tablespoons chopped mint, chives or tarragon.

GARLIC BUTTER
Add 2 crushed garlic cloves to the butter with 1–2 tablespoons chopped parsley.

ANCHOVY BUTTER
Add 6 anchovy fillets, drained of oil and mashed with a fork, to the butter. Season with pepper only.

MUSTARD BUTTER
Add 2 teaspoons English mustard and 2 tablespoons chopped chives to the butter.

These butters will keep in the refrigerator for several days, and will also freeze well, wrapped in plastic wrap or foil to prevent any loss of flavor.

Fat-Free Saffron Dip

Serve this mild dip with fresh vegetable crudités—it is particularly good with florets of cauliflower, asparagus tips and baby carrots and corn.

INGREDIENTS

1 tablespoon boiling water
small pinch saffron strands
scant 1 cup fat-free fromage frais
10 fresh chives
10 fresh basil leaves
salt and freshly ground black pepper

Serves 4

1 Pour the boiling water into a bowl and add the saffron strands. Allow to infuse for 3 minutes.

2 Beat the fromage frais in a large bowl until smooth. Stir in the infused saffron liquid with a wooden spoon.

3 Snip the chives into the dip. Tear the basil leaves into small pieces and stir them in. Mix thoroughly.

4 Add salt and freshly ground black pepper to taste. Serve the dip with fresh vegetable crudités, if desired.

Cook's Tip

If you don't have any saffron, add a squeeze of lemon or lime juice.

BASIL AND LEMON MAYONNAISE

This fresh mayonnaise is flavored with lemon and two types of basil. Serve as a dip with potato chips or crudités, or with salads and baked potatoes.

INGREDIENTS

2 egg yolks
1 tablespoon lemon juice
2/3 cup olive oil
2/3 cup sunflower oil
handful of green basil leaves
handful of opal basil leaves
4 garlic cloves, crushed
salt and freshly ground black pepper

SERVES 4

1 Place the egg yolks and lemon juice in a blender or food processor and process them briefly together.

2 In a pitcher, stir the oils together. With the machine running, pour in the oil very slowly, a drop at a time.

3 Once half the oil has been added, the remainder can be incorporated more quickly. Continue processing to form a thick, creamy mayonnaise.

4 Tear both types of basil into small pieces and stir into the mayonnaise with the crushed garlic and seasoning. Transfer to a serving dish, cover and chill until ready to serve.

SPICY YOGURT MARINADE

Use this marinade for chicken, lamb or pork, and marinate the meat, covered and chilled, for 24 to 36 hours to develop a mellow spicy flavor.

INGREDIENTS

1 teaspoon coriander seeds
2 teaspoons cumin seeds
6 cloves
2 bay leaves
1 onion, quartered
2 garlic cloves
2-inch piece fresh ginger, roughly chopped
½ teaspoon chili powder
1 teaspoon ground turmeric
⅔ cup plain yogurt
juice of 1 lemon

SERVES 6

1 Spread the coriander and cumin seeds, cloves and bay leaves over the bottom of a large frying pan and dry-fry over moderate heat until the bay leaves are crisp.

2 Allow the spices to cool, then grind coarsely with a mortar and pestle.

3 Finely chop the onion, garlic and ginger in a blender or food processor. Add the ground spices, chili powder, turmeric, yogurt and lemon juice.

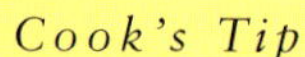

Cook's Tip

Garnish the finished dish with fresh cilantro leaves and slices of lemon or lime.

4 If you are marinating chicken parts or large pieces of meat, make several deep slashes to allow the flavors to penetrate. Arrange the pieces in a single layer and pour the marinade over them. Cover and place in the refrigerator to marinate for at least 24 hours.

Orange and Green Peppercorn Marinade

This is an excellent light marinade for delicately flavored whole fish such as sea trout, bass or bream. The beauty of the fish is perfectly set off by the softly colored marinade.

INGREDIENTS

1 red onion
2 small oranges
6 tablespoons light olive oil
2 tablespoons cider vinegar
2 tablespoons green peppercorns in brine, drained
2 tablespoons chopped fresh parsley
salt and sugar

For 1 medium-size fish

1 With a sharp knife, slash the fish 3 or 4 times on each side.

2 Cut a piece of foil big enough to wrap the fish and use to line a large dish. Peel and slice the onion and oranges. Lay half the slices on the foil, place the fish on top and cover with the remaining onion and orange.

3 Mix the remaining marinade ingredients and pour over the fish. Cover and let marinate for 4 hours, occasionally spooning the marinade over the fish.

4 Fold the foil loosely over the fish and seal the edges securely. Bake on a medium grill for 15 minutes for 1 pound, plus 15 minutes more.

Ginger and Lime Marinade

This fragrant marinade will guarantee a mouthwatering aroma from the grill. Shown here on shrimp and monkfish kebabs, it is just as delicious with chicken or pork.

INGREDIENTS

3 limes
1 tablespoon green cardamom pods
1 onion, finely chopped
1-inch piece fresh ginger, grated
1 large garlic clove, crushed
3 tablespoons olive oil

SERVES 4–6

1 Finely grate the rind from one lime and squeeze the juice from all of them.

2 Split the cardamom pods and remove the seeds. Crush with a mortar and pestle or the back of a heavy-bladed knife.

3 Mix all the marinade ingredients together and pour over the meat or fish. Stir gently, cover and set aside in a cool place to marinate for 2–3 hours.

4 Drain the meat or fish when you are ready to cook it on the grill. Baste the meat occasionally with the marinade while cooking.

SUMMER HERB MARINADE

Make the best use of summer herbs in this marinade. Try any combination of herbs, depending on what you have on hand, and use with veal, chicken, pork, lamb or salmon.

INGREDIENTS

large handful of fresh herb sprigs, e.g. chervil, thyme, parsley, sage, chives, rosemary, oregano
6 tablespoons olive oil
3 tablespoons tarragon vinegar
1 garlic clove, crushed
2 scallions, chopped
salt and freshly ground black pepper

SERVES 4

1 Discard any coarse stalks or damaged leaves from the herbs, then chop them very finely.

2 Add the chopped herbs to the remaining marinade ingredients in a large bowl. Stir to mix thoroughly.

3 Place the meat or fish in a bowl and pour the marinade over it. Cover and set aside to marinate in a cool place for 4–6 hours.

4 Drain the meat or fish when you are ready to cook it on the grill. Use the marinade to baste the meat occasionally while cooking.

Desserts

At the end of a barbecue it's a lovely idea to use the lingering fire to make a delicious fruity dessert. You can cook fruit to melting tenderness by wrapping it in foil, including sugar, spices and a sprinkling of liqueur in the parcel. To broil fruit, cut it into chunks and spear it on skewers, or just lay large slices on the grill rack. Sprinkle it with sugar to caramelize in the heat. The aroma is intoxicating: even those who thought they couldn't eat another bite will be beguiled by it. Accompany grilled fruit with a buttery, spicy sauce, crisp toasted brioche or freshly made griddle cakes – and perhaps a scoop of whipped cream or ice cream – to make a perfect end to the meal.

Grilled Apples on Cinnamon Toasts

This simple, scrumptious dessert is best made with an enriched bread such as brioche, but any light, sweet bread will do.

INGREDIENTS

4 sweet dessert apples
juice of ½ lemon
4 individual brioches or muffins
4 tablespoons melted butter
2 tablespoons raw sugar
1 teaspoon ground cinnamon
whipped cream or strained plain yogurt, to serve

Serves 4

1 Core the apples and use a sharp knife to cut them into 3 or 4 thick slices. Sprinkle the apple slices with lemon juice and set them aside.

2 Cut the brioches or muffins into thick slices. Brush the slices with melted butter on both sides.

3 Mix together the sugar and ground cinnamon in a small bowl to make the cinnamon sugar. Set aside.

4 Place the apple and brioche slices on a medium-hot grill and cook them for 3–4 minutes, turning once, until they are beginning to turn golden brown. Do not allow to burn.

5 Sprinkle half the cinnamon sugar over the apple slices and brioche toasts and grill for another minute, until the sugar is sizzling and the toasts are a rich golden brown.

6 To serve, arrange the apple slices over the toasts and sprinkle them with the remaining cinnamon sugar. Serve hot, with whipped cream or yogurt, if desired.

Pineapple Wedges with Rum Butter Glaze

Fresh pineapple is even more full of flavor when grilled, and this spiced rum glaze makes it into a very special dessert.

INGREDIENTS

1 medium pineapple
2 tablespoons dark brown sugar
1 teaspoon ground ginger
4 tablespoons melted butter
2 tablespoons dark rum

Serves 4

1 With a large, sharp knife, cut the pineapple lengthwise into 4 wedges. Cut out and discard the central core.

2 Cut between the flesh and skin, to release the skin, but leave the flesh in place. Slice the flesh across and lengthwise to make thick chunks.

3 Soak 4 bamboo skewers in water for 15 minutes to prevent them from scorching on the grill. Push a skewer through each wedge, into the stalk, to hold the chunks in place.

4 Mix together the sugar, ginger, butter and rum and brush over the pineapple. Cook the wedges on the grill for 4 minutes; pour the remaining glaze over the top and serve.

Cook's Tip

For an easier version, simply remove the skin and then cut the whole pineapple into thick slices and cook as directed.

Baked Bananas with Spicy Vanilla Filling

Bananas are ideal for barbecue cooking, as they bake in their skins and need no preparation at all. This flavored butter adds richness; children may prefer melted chocolate, jam or honey.

INGREDIENTS

4 bananas
6 green cardamom pods
1 vanilla bean
finely grated rind of 1 small orange
2 tablespoons brandy or orange juice
4 tablespoons light brown sugar
3 tablespoons butter
crème fraîche or strained plain yogurt, to serve

SERVES 4

1 Place the bananas, in their skins, on a hot grill and cook for 6–8 minutes, turning occasionally, until they are turning brownish black.

2 Meanwhile, split the cardamom pods and remove the seeds. Crush lightly with a mortar and pestle.

3 Split the vanilla bean lengthwise and scrape out the tiny seeds. Mix with the cardamom seeds, orange rind, brandy or juice, brown sugar and butter into a thick paste.

4 Using a sharp knife, slit the skin of each banana, then open out the skin and spoon in a little of the paste. Serve with a spoonful of crème fraîche or yogurt, if desired.

Oranges in Maple and Cointreau Syrup

This is one of the most delicious ways to eat an orange, and a luxurious way to round off a barbecue. For a children's or alcohol-free version, omit the liqueur.

INGREDIENTS

4 teaspoons butter, plus extra, melted, for brushing
4 medium oranges
2 tablespoons maple syrup
2 tablespoons Cointreau or Grand Marnier liqueur
crème fraîche or fromage frais, to serve

SERVES 4

1 Cut 4 double-thickness squares of aluminum foil, large enough to wrap each of the oranges. Brush the center of each square of foil with plenty of melted butter.

2 Remove some shreds of orange rind, to decorate. Blanch these, dry them and set them aside. Peel the oranges, removing all the white pith and catching the juice in a bowl.

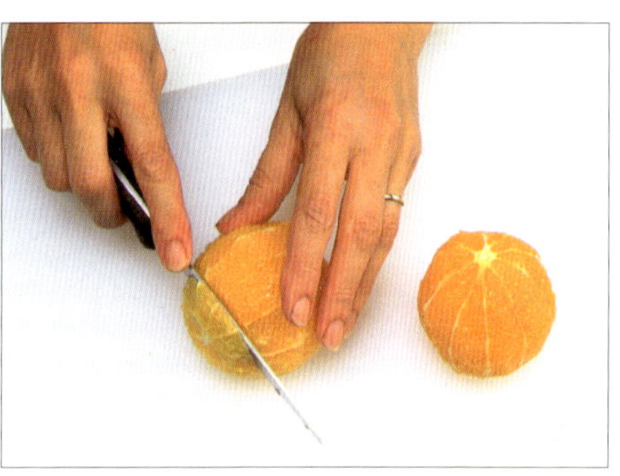

3 Slice the oranges crosswise into thick slices. Reassemble them and place each orange on a square of baking foil.

4 Tuck the foil up securely around the oranges so that they keep their shape, leaving the foil open at the top.

5 Mix together the reserved orange juice, maple syrup and liqueur and spoon the mixture over the oranges.

6 Add a pat of butter to each parcel and close the foil at the top to seal in the juices. Place the parcels on a hot grill for 10–12 minutes, until hot. Serve with crème fraîche or fromage frais, topped with the reserved shreds of orange rind.

NECTARINES WITH MARZIPAN AND MASCARPONE

A luscious dessert that no one can resist—dieters may prefer to use low-fat cream cheese or plain yogurt instead of mascarpone.

INGREDIENTS

4 firm, ripe nectarines or peaches
3 ounces marzipan
5 tablespoons mascarpone cheese
3 macaroons, crushed

SERVES 4

1 Cut the nectarines or peaches in half and remove the pits.

2 Divide the marzipan into 8 pieces, roll into balls, using your fingers, and press one piece of marzipan into the pit cavity of each nectarine half.

Cook's Tip

Either nectarines or peaches can be used for this recipe. If the pit does not pull out easily when you halve the fruit, use a small, sharp knife to cut around it.

3 Spoon the mascarpone cheese on top of the fruit halves. Sprinkle the crushed macaroons over the mascarpone.

4 Place the fruit halves on a hot grill for 3–5 minutes, until they are hot and the mascarpone starts to melt. Serve immediately.

GRILLED STRAWBERRY CROISSANTS

The combination of crisp grilled croissants, ricotta cheese and sweet strawberry preserves makes for a deliciously simple, sinful dessert.

INGREDIENTS

4 croissants
1/2 cup ricotta cheese
1/2 cup strawberry preserves or jam

SERVES 4

1 On a chopping board, split the croissants in half and open them out.

2 Spread the bottom half of each croissant with a generous layer of the ricotta cheese.

3 Top the ricotta with a generous spoonful of strawberry preserves and replace the top half of the croissant.

4 Place the filled croissants on a hot grill and cook for 2–3 minutes, turning once. Serve immediately.

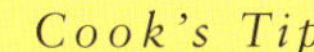

Cook's Tip

As an alternative to croissants, try scones, brioches or muffins, toasted on the grill.

GRIDDLE CAKES WITH MULLED PLUMS

These delectably light little pancakes are fun to make on the grill. They are served with a rich, spicy plum sauce.

INGREDIENTS

1¼ pounds red plums
6 tablespoons light brown sugar
1 cinnamon stick
2 whole cloves
1 piece star anise
6 tablespoons apple juice
cream or strained plain yogurt, to serve

FOR THE GRIDDLE CAKES

½ cup all-purpose flour
2 teaspoons baking powder
pinch of salt
½ cup fine cornmeal
2 tablespoons light brown sugar
1 egg, beaten
1¼ cups milk
2 tablespoons corn oil

SERVES 6

1 Halve, pit and quarter the plums. Place them in a flameproof pan, with the sugar, spices and apple juice.

Cook's Tip

If you prefer, make the griddle cakes in advance, on the stove, and then simply heat them for a few seconds on the grill to serve with the plums.

2 Bring to a boil, then reduce the heat, cover the pan and simmer gently for 8–10 minutes, stirring occasionally, until the plums are soft. Remove the spices and keep the plums warm on the side of the grill.

3 For the griddle cakes, sift the flour, baking powder and salt into a large mixing bowl and stir in the cornmeal and brown sugar.

4 Make a well in the center of the dry ingredients and add the egg, then beat in the milk. Beat thoroughly with a whisk or wooden spoon to form a smooth batter. Beat in half the oil.

5 Heat a griddle or a heavy frying pan on a hot grill. Brush with the remaining oil, then drop tablespoons of batter onto it, allowing them to spread. Cook the griddle cakes for about a minute, until bubbles start to appear on the surface and the underside is golden brown.

6 Turn the cakes over and cook the other side for a minute more, or until golden. Serve the cakes hot from the griddle with a spoonful of mulled plums and cream or yogurt.

FRUIT KEBABS WITH CHOCOLATE FONDUE

Fondues are always lots of fun, and the delicious ingredients used here—fresh fruit, chocolate and marshmallow—will make this recipe a popular choice with children and adults alike.

2 Mix together the butter, lemon juice and ground cinnamon and brush the mixture generously over the fruit.

3 For the fondue, place the chocolate, cream and marshmallows in a small pan and heat gently, without boiling, stirring constantly until the mixture has melted and is smooth.

INGREDIENTS

2 bananas
2 kiwi fruit
12 strawberries
1 tablespoon melted butter
1 tablespoon lemon juice
1 teaspoon ground cinnamon

FOR THE FONDUE
8 ounces semisweet chocolate
½ cup light cream
8 marshmallows
½ teaspoon vanilla extract

SERVES 4

1 Peel the bananas and cut into thick chunks. Peel the kiwi fruit and quarter them. Thread the bananas, kiwi fruit and strawberries onto 4 wooden skewers. (Soak the skewers in water for 15 minutes beforehand to prevent them scorching on the grill.)

4 Cook the kebabs on a medium-hot grill, turning once, for 2–3 minutes, or until the fruit is golden. Stir the vanilla extract into the fondue. Empty the fondue into a small bowl and serve at once, with the fruit kebabs.

INDEX

anchovies, peppers with
tomatoes and, 125
antipasto, roasted pepper, 17
apples: charbroiled apples on
cinnamon toasts, 148
artichoke hearts: roasted
pepper antipasto, 17

bacon: bacon kofta kebabs and
salad, 36
oyster and bacon brochettes,
42
sausages with prunes and
bacon, 34
trout with bacon, 92
bananas: baked bananas with
spicy vanilla filling, 151
barbecue sauce, 137
barbecues: choosing, 8–9
fuels, 10
lighting, 10
safety, 11
basil and lemon mayonnaise,
141
beef, 12
beef rib with onion sauce, 45
peppered steaks in beer and
garlic, 44
polpette with mozzarella and
tomato, 26
spicy meatballs, 18
Stilton burgers, 46
vegetable-stuffed beef rolls, 47
blackened Cajun chicken and
corn, 64
bread: ciabatta with mozzarella
and onions, 28
crostini with tomato and
anchovy, 29
roasted garlic toasts, 16
Brie parcels with almonds, 22
butter, parsley, 139

calamari with two-tomato
stuffing, 84
charcoal, 10
cheese: Brie parcels with
almonds, 22
ciabatta with mozzarella and
onions, 28
grilled goat cheese pizza, 109
potato and cheese polpette,
108
Stilton burgers, 46
sweet and sour vegetables with
paneer, 106
warm fava bean and feta
salad, 128
chicken, 12
baby chickens with lime and
chili, 66
blackened Cajun chicken and
corn, 64
chicken cooked in spices and
coconut, 72
chicken, mushroom and
cilantro pizza, 70
chicken salad with cilantro
dressing, 68
chicken wings teriyaki style,
24
chicken with herb and ricotta
stuffing, 65
chicken with pineapple, 60
citrus kebabs, 62
hot and sour chicken salad, 69
sweet and sour kebabs, 63
chorizo in olive oil, 19
ciabatta with mozzarella and
onions, 28
citrus kebabs, 62
Cointreau: oranges in maple
and Cointreau syrup, 152
corn on the cob in a garlic
butter crust, 115
crostini with tomato and
anchovy, 29
curly endive salad with bacon,
124

desserts, 146–58
dip, fat-free saffron, 140
duck, 12
duck breasts with red pepper
jelly glaze, 74
duck breasts with red plums,
75

eggplant: baby eggplant with
raisins and pine nuts, 130
grilled eggplant parcels, 110
spiced eggplant salad, 127
endive: curly endive salad with
bacon, 124

fava beans: fava bean,
mushroom and chorizo
salad, 129
warm fava bean and feta
salad, 128
fiery citrus salsa, 135
fish and seafood, 12, 80–103
fish parcels, 98
five-spice rib-stickers, 23

garlic toasts, roasted, 16
ginger and lime marinade, 144
griddle cakes with mulled
plums, 156

ham pizzettas with melted Brie
and mango, 38

jumbo shrimp skewers with
walnut pesto, 82
juniper-spiced venison chops,
56

kebabs: bacon kofta kebabs and
salad, 36
citrus kebabs, 62
fruit kebabs with chocolate
fondue, 158
mackerel kebabs with sweet
pepper salad, 88
shish kebab, 35
sweet and sour kebabs, 63
vegetable kebabs with
peppercorn sauce, 107
kofta kebabs, bacon, 36

lamb, 12
grilled lamb with potato slices,
52
lamb burgers with red currant
chutney, 50
lamb with lavender balsamic
marinade, 54
lamb with mint and lemon, 55
shish kebab, 35
skewered lamb with cilantro
yogurt, 49
skewered lamb with red onion
salsa, 27

mackerel: mackerel kebabs with
sweet pepper salad, 88
mackerel with tomatoes, pesto
and onion, 93
maple syrup: oranges in maple
and Cointreau syrup, 152
marinades, 13
ginger and lime, 144
orange and green peppercorn,
143
spicy yogurt, 142
summer herb, 145
mayonnaise, basil and lemon,

141
meatballs: polpette with
mozzarella and tomato, 26
spicy meatballs, 18
Mediterranean turkey skewers,
73
Mexican barbecued salmon,
102
mixed grill skewers with
horseradish sauce, 32
monkfish with peppered citrus
marinade, 96
mushrooms: chicken,
mushroom and
cilantro pizza, 70
fava bean, mushroom and
chorizo salad, 129
lemongrass pork chops with
mushrooms, 43

nectarines with marzipan and
mascarpone, 154

onions: beef rib with onion
sauce, 45
caramelized onion relish, 138
skewered lamb with red onion
salsa, 27
sweet and sour onion salad,
126
oranges: fiery citrus salsa, 135
orange and green peppercorn
marinade, 143
oranges in maple and
Cointreau syrup, 152
oyster and bacon brochettes, 42

parsley butter, 139

peppered steaks in beer and
garlic, 44
peppers: charbroiled tuna with
fiery pepper purée, 86
mackerel kebabs with sweet
pepper salad, 88
peppers with tomatoes
and anchovies, 125
roasted pepper antipasto, 17
pheasant with sage and lemon,
76
pineapple: chicken with
pineapple, 60
pineapple wedges with rum
butter glaze, 150
pizzas: chicken, mushroom and
cilantro pizza, 70
goat cheese pizza, 109
ham pizzettas with melted Brie
and mango, 38
polenta, herb, 20
polpette: potato and cheese, 108
with mozzarella and tomato,
26
pork, 12
five-spice rib-stickers, 23
lemongrass pork chops with
mushrooms, 43
pork and pineapple satay, 40
potatoes: grilled lamb with
potato slices, 52
potato and cheese polpette,
108
potato skewers with mustard
dip, 120
potato wedges with garlic and
rosemary, 121
poultry, 58–79
prunes, sausages with bacon
and, 34

quail with a five-spice
marinade, 78

radicchio, artichoke and walnut
salad, 131
red mullet with basil and citrus,
95
red snapper: spiced fish baked
Thai style, 94

saffron dip, fat-free, 140
salads, 36, 69, 122–31
salmon, Mexican barbecued,
102
salsas: chunky cherry tomato,
134
fiery citrus, 135
fresh corn, 136
sardines with warm herb salsa,
85
sauce, barbecue, 137
sausages with prunes and
bacon, 34
scallops: grilled scallops
with lime butter, 90
sea bass: fish parcels, 98
grilled sea bass with citrus
fruit, 100
grilled sea bass with fennel,
101
seafood and fish, 12, 80–103
shish kebab, 35
shrimp: jumbo shrimp
skewers with walnut pesto, 82
spiced shrimp with
vegetables, 83
spare ribs: five-spice rib-
stickers, 23
spiced fish baked Thai style, 94
spinach with raisins and pine
nuts, 113
squash: baked squash with
Parmesan, 116
squid: calamari with two-
tomato stuffing, 84
Stilton burgers, 46
strawberry croissants, grilled,
155
sweet and sour kebabs, 63
sweet and sour onion salad,
126
sweet and sour vegetables with
paneer, 106

tofu steaks, 25

tomatoes: barbecue sauce, 137
calamari with two-tomato
stuffing, 84
chunky cherry tomato salsa,
134
crostini with tomato and
anchovy, 29
mackerel with tomatoes, pesto
and onion, 93
peppers with tomatoes
and anchovies, 125
trout with bacon, 92
tuna: charbroiled tuna with
fiery pepper purée, 86
turkey skewers, Mediterranean,
73

veal chops with basil butter, 48
vegetables: summer vegetables
with yogurt pesto, 118
sweet and sour vegetables with
paneer, 106
vegetable kebabs with
peppercorn sauce, 107
vegetable parcels with flowery
butter, 112
vegetable-stuffed beef rolls, 47
vegetarian dishes, 104–21
venison chops, juniper-spiced,
56

yogurt marinade, spicy, 142

zucchini, baked stuffed, 114